Data Structures Through C++

Third Edition

Yashavant P. Kanetkar

FIRST EDITION 2019

Copyright © BPB Publications, INDIA
ISBN : 978-93-8851-136-0

Distributors:

BPB PUBLICATIONS
20, Ansari Road, Darya Ganj
New Delhi-110002
Ph: 23254990/23254991

BPB BOOK CENTRE
376 Old Lajpat Rai Market,
Delhi-110006
Ph: 23861747

MICRO MEDIA
Shop No. 5, Mahendra Chambers, 150
DN Rd. Next to Capital Cinema, V.T.
(C.S.T.) Station,
MUMBAI-400 001
Ph: 22078296/22078297

DECCAN AGENCIES
4-3-329, Bank Street,
Hyderabad-500195
Ph: 24756967/24756400

Published by Manish Jain for BPB Publications, 20, Ansari Road, Darya Ganj, New Delhi- 110002 and Printed him at Repro India Pvt Ltd, Mumbai

Dedicated to
Prabhakar Kanetkar

About the Author

Through his books and Quest Video Courseware DVDs on C, C++, Data Structures, VC++, .NET, Embedded Systems, etc. Yashavant Kanetkar has created, moulded and groomed lacs of IT careers in the last two and half decades. Yashavant's books and Quest DVDs have made a significant contribution in creating top-notch IT manpower in India and abroad.

Yashavant's books are globally recognized and millions of students / professionals have benefitted from them. Yashavant's books have been translated into Hindi, Gujarati, Japanese, Korean and Chinese languages. Many of his books are published in India, USA, Japan, Singapore, Korea and China.

Yashavant is a much sought after speaker in the IT field and has conducted seminars/workshops at TedEx, IITs, RECs and global software companies.

Yashavant has been honored with the prestigious "Distinguished Alumnus Award" by IIT Kanpur for his entrepreneurial, professional and academic excellence. This award was given to top 50 alumni of IIT Kanpur who have made significant contribution towards their profession and betterment of society in the last 50 years.

In recognition of his immense contribution to IT education in India, he has been awarded the "Best .NET Technical Contributor" and "Most Valuable Professional" awards by Microsoft for 5 successive years.

Yashavant holds a BE from VJTI Mumbai and M.Tech. from IIT Kanpur. Yashavant's current affiliations include being a Director of KICIT Pvt. Ltd. and KSET Pvt. Ltd.

Acknowledgments

Though what matters most in a book are its contents, it is the parts of the whole like cover, internal layout, digital extras, price etc. that make it an attractive proposition. I have been fortunate to get help and cooperation from many individuals involved in this book project.

Though the book cover bears only my name, it truly reflects the collective wisdom of numerous students to whom I taught "Data Structures" for several years. I have learnt a lot from them. Many thanks, wherever you are.

Writing and testing programs in a book is a monumental task calling for incredible patience. That Vineeta Prasad, Anil Gakhare and Monali Mohadikar had loads of it is chiefly responsible for getting the book in its current form. They also ensured that we chose the right algorithms while implementing the additional programs present in the downloadable DVD.

"Experience data structures through animations"—that is the main theme of this book. Neeraj Srivastav took the responsibility of creating excellent animations while following stringent timelines. M.S. Prakash wrote instructions for installing and using the programs on the DVD. Many thanks to both of you.

An author needs a lot of support from his publisher. That Manish Jain of BPB provides in abundance in my every book project. Bureaucracy and quiet indifference are the words which do not figure in his dictionary.

And lastly many thanks to my wife Seema who cheered me in good times, encouraged me in bad times and understood me at all times. If I ever wear a hat, it would be off to her!!

Contents

Introduction

Technical book writing is a simple job. Pick a topic that appeals to you, spend some time understanding it, browse the net for some additional information and then keep writing till the time you do not reach the end. Easier said than done!

In fact nothing can be farther from the truth. For one, choosing the right subject is pretty confusing with so many subjects and technologies taking so big strides in the recent years. Secondly, none of them is so easy to master in a few months and thirdly presenting what you have understood in a simple manner is not everybody's cup of tea.

I have realized all these facts more emphatically while writing this book, because I have been writing this book for last 10 years!! It all began with attempting to write articles that would explain Quick Sort algorithm and Threaded Binary Trees. Once I had a critical mass of written material I thought of compiling it in the form of a book.

I however wanted the book to be a *different* data structures book. Different in the sense that, it should go beyond merely explaining how typical data structures like stacks, queues and linked lists work. I wanted the readers to *experience* sorting of an array, traversing of a doubly linked list, construction of a binary tree, etc.

I had a hell of a time imagining, understanding and programming these complicated data structures. I wanted that the readers of this book should not be required to undergo that agony. And today I am satisfied that I have been able to achieve this through the downloadable DVD. It lets the reader experience the working of different data structures through carefully prepared animations. I have pinned my hopes that the readers would appreciate this approach.

I have tried to make this book different in one more way. Instead of merely learning how to perform different operations on a linked list, I think one can appreciate it better if one comes to the practical applications of it. There are numerous such examples and I have also tried to provide animations for most of them on the downloadable DVD.

Apart from this I have tried to explain all data structures with examples and figures. I have also provided exercises at the end of each chapter to hone your skills.

In the 3rd edition I have done a major overhaul of all chapters. I have made the Analysis of Algorithms chapter more comprehensible by explaining this difficult topic with numerous examples. I hope the readers would like this approach.

I have also eliminated those algorithms and programs that are not commonly used and are of only academic importance. In this edition you would also find a lot consistency in the style of programming adopted while implementing different algorithms.

Yashavant Kanetkar

Analysis of
Algorithms

Justifying the means

Why This Chapter Matters?

The dictum "ends justify the means" doesn't hold good in Computer Science. Just because we got the right answer (end) does not mean that the method (means) that we employed to obtain it was correct. In fact, the efficiency of obtaining the correct answer is largely dependent on the method employed to obtain it. Hence scientific analysis of performance of the method is very important.

The method of solving a problem is known as an algorithm. More precisely, an algorithm is a sequence of instructions that act on some input data to produce desired output in a finite number of steps. An algorithm must have the following properties:

(a) Input – An algorithm must receive some input data supplied externally.

(b) Output – An algorithm must produce at least one output as the result.

(c) Finiteness – No matter what the input might be, the algorithm must terminate after a finite number of steps. For example, a procedure which goes on performing a series of steps infinitely is not an algorithm.

(d) Definiteness – The steps to be performed in the algorithm must be clear and unambiguous.

(e) Effectiveness – One must be able to perform the steps in the algorithm without applying any intelligence. For example, the step—Select three numbers which form a Pythagorean triplet—is not effective.

Why Analyze Algorithms?

Multiple algorithms may exist for solving a given problem. To determine which algorithm is more efficient than others, we need to analyze the algorithms. This analysis is done by comparing the time and/or space required for executing the algorithms. In this chapter we would analyze algorithms on the basis of time. We would carry out space based analysis in later chapters.

While doing time based analysis of algorithms we do not use conventional time units like seconds or minutes required for executing the algorithms. There are two reasons for this.

(a) A worse algorithm may take less time units to execute if we move it to a faster computer, or use a more efficient language.

(b) We are interested in relative efficiency of different algorithms rather than the exact time for one.

So instead of time units we consider the number of prominent operations that are carried out by the algorithm. For example, in a searching algorithm we would try to determine the number of comparisons that are done to search a value in a list of values. Or in an algorithm to add two matrices, we might determine the number of arithmetic operations it performs.

Once we identify the prominent operations in an algorithm, we try to build a function that relates this number of operations to the size of the input. Once these functions are formed for algorithms under consideration, we can compare them by comparing the rate at which the functions grow as the input gets larger. This growth rate is critical since there are situations where one algorithm needs fewer operations than the other when the input size is small, but many more when the input size becomes larger.

Thus analysis of algorithms gives us a scientific reason to determine which algorithm should be chosen to solve the problem.

What to Consider, What to Ignore?

It is very important to decide which operations to consider and which operations to ignore while analyzing an algorithm. For this we must first identify which is the significant time consuming operation(s) in the algorithm. Once that is decided, we should determine which of these operations are integral to the algorithm and which merely contribute to the overheads. There are two classes of operations that are typically chosen for the significant operation—comparison or arithmetic.

For example, in Searching and Sorting algorithms the important task being done is the comparison of two values. While searching the comparison is done to check if the value is the one we are looking for, whereas in sorting the comparison is done to see whether values being compared are out of order.

The arithmetic operations fall under two groups—additive and multiplicative. Additive operators include addition, subtraction, increment, and decrement. Multiplicative operators include multiplication, division, and modulus. These two groups are counted separately because multiplication operations take longer time to execute than additions.

Let us now see which operations we should ignore while analyzing an algorithm. Suppose we have an algorithm that counts the number of characters in a file. This algorithm is given below.

Count = 0

While there are more characters in the file do
    Increment Count by 1
    Get the next character
End while
Print Count

If there are 500 characters present in the file we need to initialize **Count** once, check the condition 500 + 1 times (the +1 is for the last check when the file is empty), and increment the counter 500 times. Thus the total number of operations would be

Initializations – 1
Increments – 500
Conditional checks – 500 + 1
Printing – 1

As can be seen from these numbers, the number of increments and conditional checks are far too many as compared to number of initialization and printing operations. The number of initialization and printing operations would remain same for a file of any size and they become a much smaller percentage of the total as the file size increases. For a large file, the number of initialization and printing operations would be insignificant as compared to the number of increments and conditional checks. Thus, while analyzing this algorithm the initialization operation should be ignored.

Cases to Consider During Analysis

Choosing the input to consider when analyzing an algorithm can have a significant impact on how an algorithm will perform. For example, if the input list is already sorted, some sorting algorithms will perform very well, but other sorting algorithms may perform very poorly. The opposite may be true if the list is randomly arranged instead of sorted. Hence, multiple input sets must be considered while analyzing an algorithm. These include the following:

(a) Best Case Input – This represents the input set that allows an algorithm to perform quickest, i.e. this input the algorithm takes shortest time to execute, as it causes the algorithms to do the least amount of work. For example, for a searching algorithm the best case would be if the value we are searching for is found in the first location that the search algorithm checks. As a result, this algorithm would need only one comparison irrespective of the complexity of the algorithm. No matter how large is the input, searching in a best case will result in a constant time. Since possibility of best case input for an algorithm would usually be very small, the best case analysis of an algorithm is often not done.

(b) Worst Case Input – This represents the input set that allows an algorithm to perform slowest. Worst case is an important analysis because it gives us an idea of the maximum time an algorithm will ever take. Worst case analysis requires that we identify the input values that cause an algorithm to do the most work. For example, for a searching algorithm, the worst case is one where the value is in the last place we check or is not in the list. This could involve comparing the key to each list value for a total of N comparisons.

(c) Average Case Input – This represents the input set that allows an algorithm to deliver an average performance. Average-case analysis is a four-step process. These steps are as under:

1. Determine the number of different groups into which all possible input sets can be divided.
2. Determine the probability that the input will come from each of these groups.
3. Determine how long the algorithm will run for each of these groups. All of the input in each group should take the same amount of time, and if they do not, the group must be split into two separate groups.
4. Calculate average case time using the formula:

$$A(n) = \sum_{i=1}^{m} p_i * t_i$$

where,

n = Size of input
m = Number of groups
p_i = Probability that the input will be from group i
t_i = Time that the algorithm takes for input from group i.

Rates of Growth

While analyzing algorithms, more than the exact number of operations performed by the algorithm, it is the rate of increase in operations as the size of the problem increases that is of more importance. This is often called the rate of growth of the algorithm. What happens with small sets of input data is not as interesting as what happens when the data set gets large.

Table 1-1 shows rate of growth for some of the common classes of algorithms for a wide range of input sizes. You can observe that there isn't a significant difference in values when the input is small, but once the input value gets large, there are big differences. Hence, while analyzing algorithms, we must consider what happens when the size of the input is large, because small input sets can hide rather dramatic differences.

n	log n	n log n	n^2	n^3	2^n
1	0.0	0.0	1.0	1.0	2.0
2	1.0	2.0	4.0	8.0	4.0
5	2.3	11.6	25.0	125.0	32.0
10	3.3	33.2	100.0	1000.0	1024.0
15	3.9	58.6	225.0	3375.0	32768.0
20	4.3	86.4	400.0	8000.0	1048576.0
30	4.9	147.2	900.0	27000.0	1073741824.0
40	5.3	212.9	1600.0	64000.0	1099511627776.0
50	5.6	282.2	2500.0	125000.0	1125899906842620.0

Table 1-1. *Rate of increase in common algorithm classes.*

The data in Table 1-1 also illustrates that the faster growing functions increase at such a rate that they quickly dominate the slower-growing functions. Thus, if the algorithm's complexity is a combination of a two of these classes, we can safely ignore the slower growing terms. On discarding these terms, we are left with what we call the order of the function or related algorithm. We usually consider one algorithm to be more efficient than another if its worst case running time has a lower order of growth.

Based on their order, algorithms can be grouped into three categories:

(a) Algorithms that grow at least as fast as some function

(b) Algorithms that grow no faster

(c) Algorithms that grow at the same rate

The categories (a), (b), (c) mentioned above are commonly represented using Asymptotic Notations Big Omega Ω (g(n)), Big Oh O (g(n)) and Big Theta θ (g(n)), respectively. These notations are discussed below in detail.

Asymptotic Notation for Analysis of Algorithms

The Big Omega category of functions are not of much interest to us since for all values of **n** greater than some threshold value n_0 all the functions in Ω have values that are at least as large as **g**. That is, all functions in this category grow as fast as **g** or even faster. Using Asymptotic Notation this is represented as

$f (n) >= c g (n)$

where **c** is some constant > 0 and n >= n_0 >= 1.

Thus **g(n)** represents the best case or the lower bound. If there are positive constants n_0 and **c** such that at and to the right of n_0, value of **f(n)** always lies on or above **g(n)**. This relationship has been shown graphically in Figure 1-1 (a).

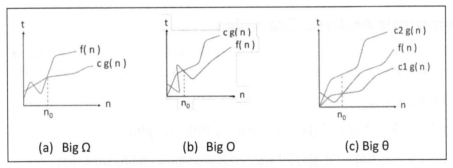

(a) Big Ω (b) Big O   (c) Big θ

Figure 1-1. *Asymptotic representation of functions.*

The Big Oh class of functions would be of interest to us as it represents the class of functions that grow no faster than **g**. This means that for all values of **n** greater than some threshold n_0, all the functions in O have values that are no greater than **g**. Thus **g(n)** represents the worst case or upper bound. So, none of the functions in this class grow faster than **g**. Using Asymptotic Notation this is represented as

$f (n) <= c g (n)$

where **c** is some constant > 0 and n >= n_0 >= 1.

Thus **if** there are positive constants n_0 and **c** such that at and to the right of n_0, value of **f(n)** always lies on or below **g(n)**. This relationship has been shown graphically in Figure 1-1 (b).

Big Theta represents the class of functions that are bounded by **g(n)** on either side. This means that for all values of **n** greater than some threshold n_0, all the functions in **θ** have values that are greater than $c_1g(n)$ and less than $c_2g(n)$. Using Asymptotic Notation, this is represented as

$$c_1 g(n) <= f(n) <= c_2 g(n)$$

where c_1 **and** c_2 are some constants > 0 and n >= n_0 >= 1.

Thus, if there are positive constants n_0, c_1 **and** c_2 such that at and to the right of n_0, value of **f(n)** always is bounded by **g(n)** on either side. This relationship has been shown graphically in Figure 1-1 (c).

While analyzing algorithms we are on the lookout for an algorithm that does better than the one that we are considering. Since big theta category represents a class of functions that grow at the same rate as the function **g** this category is usually not of interest to us.

Asymptotic Analysis Examples

Let us now see some examples of asymptotic analysis that we learnt above. We would consider one example of each category— Ω, O and θ.

Example 1-1

If **f(n) = 5n + 3** and **g(n) = n**, can we say **f(n) = Ω (g(n))**?

We can say **f(n) = Ω(g(n))** if we can find some **c** and n_0 such that

f(n) >= c g(n), c > 0, n > n_0, >= 1.

Substituting **f(n)** and **g(n)** in this expression, we get

5n + 3 >= cn

This equation is satisfied, for **c = 1** and for all values of **n >= 1**.

So we can say for **c = 1, n_0 = 1, f(n) = Ω(g(n))**

Note that **g(n)** can also be **log n** or **log log n** which grow slower than **n**. But tightest lower bound is **n**. So **f(n) = Ω(n)**.

Example 1-2

If $f(n) = 5n + 3$ and $g(n) = n$, can we say $f(n) = O(g(n))$?

We can say $f(n) = O(g(n))$ if we can find some c and n_0 such that

$f(n) <= c\ g(n)$, where $c > 0, n > n_0 >= 1$.

Substituting $f(n)$ and $g(n)$ in this expression, we get

$5n + 3 <= cn$

This equation is satisfied, for $c = 6$ and for all value of $n >= 3$.

So for $c = 6, n_0 = 3, f(n) = O(g(n))$

Note that $g(n)$ can also be $n^3, n^2, 2^n$ which grow faster than n, But tightest upper bound is n. So $f(n) = O(n)$.

Example 1-3

If $f(n) = 5n + 3$ and $g(n) = n$, can we say $f(n) = \theta(g(n))$?

We can say $f(n) = \theta(g(n))$ if we can find some c_1, c_2 and n_0 such that

$c_1 g(n) <= f(n) <= c_2 g(n)$, where $c_1, c_2 > 0, n > n_0 >= 1$.

Substituting $f(n)$ and $g(n)$ in this expression, we get

$c_1 n <= 5n + 3 <= c_2 n$

This inequality is satisfied, for $c_1 = 1, c_2 = 6$ and for all value of $n >= 3$.

So for $c_1 = 1, c2 = 6, n_0 = 3, f(n) = \theta(g(n))$

Is Asymptotic Analysis Perfect?

Suppose two algorithms have rate of growth represented by functions **100nlog n** and **2nlog n** respectively. Ignoring the constants order of growth of both algorithms would be **nlog n**. So both algorithms are asymptotically same. Hence we can't judge which one is better.

While doing Asymptotic Analysis we always consider input size n greater than some constant value n_0. But, in reality, we may never supply input bigger than n_0. In such cases, an asymptotically slower algorithm may perform better than an asymptotically faster algorithm.

From these examples we can conclude that asymptotic analysis is not perfect, but it still remains the best way available. Hence, it is widely used while analyzing algorithms.

Comparison of Growth Rates

Comparison of some growth rates is obvious. For example, we can intuitively say n^3 grows faster than n^2, which grows faster than **n**. But we may not be so sure when we compare growth rates of function 2^n and n^2. In such cases we need to follow following steps:

(a) If anything is common, cancel it out

(b) Take log of both sides and then compare

(c) Replace **n** with some large value of power of 2

(d) Compare the two functions

Note that if functions differ by constant value, then asymptotically they are same; they differ only in actual value.

Let us take a few examples to fix our ideas.

Example 1-4

Which of the following two functions is greater?

$f(n) = 2^n$ and $g(n) = n^2$

Take log of both functions

$n \log_2 2$	$2 \log_2 n$
n	$2 * \log_2 n$
2^{100}	$2 * \log_2 2^{100}$
2^{100}	$2 * 100$
2^{100}	200

So, **g(n) < f(n)**. Or in other words we can say **g(n) = O(f(n))**.

Example 1-5

Which of the following two functions is greater?

$f(n) = 3^n$ and $g(n) = 2^n$

Take log of both sides

$n \log_2 3$	$n \log_2 2$
$\log_2 3$	$\log_2 2$

So, $g(n) < f(n)$

$g(n) = O(f(n))$

Example 1-6

Which of the following two functions is greater?

$f(n) = n^2$ and $g(n) = n \log_2 n$

Cancel out **n**

n^2	$n \log_2 n$
n	$\log_2 n$

So, $g(n) < f(n)$

$g(n) = O(\,f(n)\,)$

Example 1-7

Which of the following two functions is greater?

$f(n) = n$ and $g(n) = (\log_2 n)^{100}$

Take log of both functions

$\log_2 n$	$100 * \log_2 \log_2 n$

Substitute $n = 2^{128}$

$\log_2 2^{128}$	$100 * \log_2 \log_2 2^{128}$
128	$100 * \log_2 128$
128	$100 * \log_2 2^7$
128	$100 * 7$

So, **f(n) < g(n)**

Let us substitute $n = 2^{1024}$

$\log_2 2^{1024}$	$100 * \log \log 2^{1024}$
1024	$100 * \log 1024$
1024	$100 * \log 2^{10}$
1024	$100 * 10$
1024	1000

So, **f(n) > g(n)**

So, after some value of **n, f(n) > g(n)**

Example 1-8

Which of the following two functions is greater?

If $f(n) = n^{\log n}$ and $g(n) = n \log n$

Take log of both functions

log n * log n   log n + log log n

Substitute n = 2^{1024}

log 2^{1024} log 2^{1024} log 2^{1024} + log log 2^{1024}
1024 * 1024   1024 + 10
So, **f(n) > g(n)**

Determining Time Complexity

From the Asymptotic Analysis discussed previously, we know that we would be interested in Big O as it represents the worst case time complexity. So, let us take a few examples to calculate the time complexity. Note that the functions in the following examples are in pseudo code form and not as syntactically correct C++ code.

Example 1-9

```
fun( )
{
    int i ;
    for ( i = 1 to n )
        printf ( "Hello\n" ) ;
}
```

Here **printf( )** would be executed **n** times so time complexity is **O(n)**.

Example 1-10

```
fun( )
{
    int i, j ;
    for ( i = 1 to n )
    {
        for ( j = 1 to n )
            printf ( "Hello\n" ) ;
    }
}
```

Here **printf( )** would be executed n^2 times so time complexity is **O(n^2)**.

Example 1-11

```
fun( int n )
{
    int i = 1 ;
    for ( i = 1 ; i * i <= n ; i++ )
```

```
        printf ( "Hello\n" ) ;
}
```

The condition used in the loop **i * i <= n**, which is same as **i <= √n**. So **printf( )** would get executed **√n** times. So time complexity is **O (√n)**.

Example 1-12

```
fun ( int n )
{
    int i = 1, s = 1 ;
    while ( s <= n )
    {
        i++ ;
        s = s + i ;
        printf ( "Hello\n" ) ;
    }
}
```

Here we can't say that the loop would be executed **n** times because value of **s** is being incremented in steps of **i** and not in steps of 1. In this function values of **i** and **s** would get incremented as per the following pattern:

$i = 1, 2, 3, 4, 5, ..., k$

$s = 1, 3, 6, 10, 15, 21, ...$

By the time **s** becomes greater than **n**, loop would go around **k** times.

When i = 1, s = sum of first 1 Natural numbers
When i = 2, s = sum of first 2 Natural numbers
When i = 3, s = sum of first 3 Natural numbers

...

When i = k, s = sum of first k Natural numbers.

When loop stops **s > n.**

This means

$k (k + 1) / 2 > n$

or $(k^2 + k) / 2 > n$

Ignoring the lower order terms $k^2 > n$

So, number of iterations **k** will be **√n**

So, time complexity is **O (√n).**

Example 1-13

```
fun ( int n )
{
    int i, j, k ;
    for ( i = 1 ; i <= n ; i++ )
    {
        for ( j = 1 ; j <= i ; j++ )
        {
            for ( k = 1 ; i <= 50 ; i++ )
                printf ( "Hello\n" ) ;
        }
    }
}
```

Let us analyse how many times each loop in this function gets executed.

For i = 1, j loop executes 1 time and k loop executes 50 times.
For i = 2, j loop executes 2 times and k loop executes 2 * 50 times.
For i = 3, j loop executes 3 times and k loop executes 3 * 50 times.
For i = n, j loop executes n times and k loop executes n * 50 times.

So, **printf( )** would get executed

50 + 2 * 50 + 3 * 50 + ... + n * 50 times
= 50 * (1 + 2 + 3 + ... + n) times
= 50 * n (n + 1) / 2) times

Ignoring the lower order terms and the coefficients, time complexity would be $O (n^2)$.

Example 1-14

```
fun ( int n )
{
    int i ;
    for ( i = 1 ; i < n ; i = i * 2 )
        printf ( "Hello\n" ) ;
}
```

In this function the value of **i** is incremented as per the following pattern:

i = 1, 2, 4, 8, 16,... n
Or
$i = 2^0, 2^1, 2^2, 2^3, 2^4, ... 2^k$

When all iterations are over 2^k would be equal to **n**. So **k** would be equal to **log₂ n**. So **printf( )** would get executed **log₂ n** times. Hence time complexity would be **O (log₂ n)**.

Note that had the incrementation been done using the expression **i = i * 3**, time complexity would be **O (log₃ n)**. Likewise, had it been done using **i = i * 4**, time complexity would be **O (log₄ n)**.

Types of Algorithms

Though the problems might be very different it is possible that the algorithms used to solve them are similar. For example, the two problems—counting elements in a list and checking whether a value exists in a list are different. Still the algorithms for both are very similar. Hence algorithms are often classified as per their characteristics rather than the problem that they are attempting to solve. Given below is a list of some common types of algorithms. I do not intend to explain characteristics of these algorithms here. Some of them are explained in chapters to follow.

(a) Iterative algorithms

(b) Recursive algorithms

(c) Backtracking algorithms

(d) Divide and conquer algorithms

(e) Dynamic programming algorithms

(f) Greedy algorithms

(g) Branch and bound algorithms

(h) Brute force algorithms

(i) Randomized algorithms

Chapter Bullets

Summary of chapter

(a) Algorithm is a method of accomplishing a task in a finite number of steps.

(b) An algorithm must have input, output, finiteness, definiteness and effectiveness.

(c) Analysis of an algorithm involves determining time requirement or memory space requirement.

(d) Asymptotic analysis evaluates an algorithm's performance in terms of input size. It calculates how time / space increases with input size.

(e) Asymptotic notation describes 3 rates of growth Big Ω, Big O and Big θ.

(f) Usually Big O analysis of an algorithm is done, as it determines the worst case time complexity.

(g) Though Asymptotic Analysis is not perfect, it is still the best way available to analyze algorithm's performance.

(h) Time complexity of a function can be found out by determining the number of times the dominant operation is being performed in the function.

(i) Order of growth of two functions can be compared by taking log of functions and substituting a large value in place of n.

Check Your Progress

Exercise - Level I

[A] Pick up the correct alternative for each of the following questions:

(a) If algorithm A1 is asymptotically more efficient than algorithm A2, then which of the following statement is correct?

    (1) A1 would be more efficient for all inputs
    (2) A1 would be more efficient for all inputs except small inputs
    (3) A1 would be more efficient for all inputs except large inputs
    (4) A2 would be more efficient for small inputs

(b) The correct increasing order of Asymptotic complexity of 4 functions given below is

    fun1 (n) = 2^n
    fun2 (n) = $n^{3/2}$
    fun3 (n) = nlog n
    fun4 (n) = n^ (log n)

    (1) fun3, fun2, fun4, fun1

(2) fun3, fun2, fun1, fun4
(3) fun2, fun3, fun1, fun4
(4) fun2, fun3, fun4, fun1

(c) Four functions **fun1( )**, **fun2( )**, **fun3( )** and **fun4( )** use four different for loops given below, where n > 0.

```
for ( i = 0 ; i < n ; i++ )
for ( i = 0 ; i < n ; i += 2 )
for ( i = 1 ; i < n ; i *= 2 )
for ( i = n ; i > -1 ; i /= 2 )
```

Which function would be most efficient?

(1) fun1
(2) fun2
(3) fun3
(4) fun4

(d) Which of the following is not $O(n^2)$?
(1) $12^5 * n + 12099$
(2) $n^{3.14}$
(3) $3^{10} * n$
(4) $n^3 / \sqrt{n}$

(e) Consider the following function fun( ):

```
double fun ( int n )
{
    int i ;
    double sum ;
    if ( n = = 0 )
        return 1.0 ;
    else
    {
        sum = 0.0 ;
        for ( i = 0 ; i < n ; i++ )
            sum += fun ( i ) ;
        return sum ;
    }
}
```

The time complexity of the above function is:

(1) O (1)

   (2) O (n)
   (3) O (n!)
   (4) O (nn)

(f) Consider the following function with n >= m.

```
int gcd ( int n, int m )
{
      if ( n % m == 0 )
            return m ;

      n = n % m ;

      return gcd ( m, n ) ;
}
```

   How many recursive calls are made in the above function?

   (1) θ (log n)
   (2) Ω (n)
   (3) θ (log log n)
   (4) θ (sqrt (n))

[B] Two different procedures are written for a given problem. One has a computing time given by 2^n and that for the other is n^3. Specify the range of n for which each would be suitable.

[C] Compare the two functions n^2 and $2^n / 4$ for various values for *n*. Determine when the second becomes larger than the first.

[D] Which of the following function grow faster?

   i. $\sqrt{n}$ or log n ?
   ii. $n^{\log n}$ or $\log n^n$?

   Prove your claim.

Sharpen Your Skills

Exercise - Level II

[E] Determine the time complexity of the following algorithms:

(a) fun(int n)
      {

```
        int old, new, term, n ;
        old = new = 1 ;
        printf ( "%d %d ", old, new ) ;
        for ( i = 1 ; i <= n ; i++ )
        {
                term = old + new ;
                printf ( "%d ", term ) ;
                old = new ;
                new = term ;
        }
    }
(b)  fun ( int n )
    {
        for ( i = 1 ; i<= n ; i++ )
        {
                for ( j = 1 ; j <= i ; j++ )
                {
                        for ( k = 1 ; k <= j ; k++ )
                        printf ( "Hello\n" ) ;
                }
        }
    }
(c)  fun ( int n )
    {
        i = 1 ;
        while ( i <= n )
        {
                x++ ;
                i++ ;
        }
    }
(d)  int fun ( int n )
    {
        int i, j, count = 0 ;
        for ( i = n ; i > 0 ; i /= 2 )
        {
                for ( j = 0 ; j < i ; j++ )
                        count = count + 1 ;
        }
        return count ;
```

```
        }
(e)  int fun ( int n )
     {
            int i, j, count = 0 ;
            for ( i = 0 ; i < n ; i++ )
            {
                 for ( j = i ; j > 0 ; j-- )
                     count = count + 1 ;
            }
            return count ;
     }

(f)  fun ( int n )
     {
            int i, j = 0 ;
            for ( i = 0 ; i < n ; ++i )
            {
                 while ( j < n )
                     j++ ;
            }
     }

(g)  int fun ( int n )
     {
            int i, j, k = 0 ;
            for ( i = n / 2 ; i <= n ; i++ )
            {
                 for ( j = 2 ; j <= n ; j = j * 2 )
                     k = k + n/2 ;
            }
            return k ;
     }

(h)  fun ( int n )
     {
            int j ;
            j = 1 ;
            while ( j <= n )
            {
                 j = j * 2 ;
                 printf ( "Hello\n" ) ;
            }
```

```
         }
(i)   fun ( int n )
      {
             int i, j ;
             for ( i = n, j = 0 ; i > 0 ; i /= 2, j += i )
                   printf ( "Hello\n" ) ;
      }

(j)   fun ( int n )
      {
             int i, j, k ;
             for ( i = 1 ; i <= n ; i++ )
                   for ( j = i ; j <= n ; j++ )
                         for ( k = j + 1 ; k <= n ; k++ )
                               printf ( "Hello\n" ) ;
      }

(k)   fun ( int n )
      {
             int i, j, k ;
             for ( i = 1 ; i <= n ; i++ )
             {
                   for ( j = 1 ; j <= i * i ; j++ )
                   {
                         for ( k = 1 ; i <= n/2 ; i++ )
                               printf ( "Hello\n" ) ;
                   }
             }
      }

(l)   fun ( int n )
      {
             int i, j, k ;
             for ( i = n/2 ; i <= n ; i++ )
             {
                   for ( j = 1 ; j <= n/2 ; j++ )
                   {
                         for ( k = 1 ; i <= n ; k = k*2 )
                               printf ( "Hello\n" ) ;
                   }
             }
      }
```

(m)
```
fun ( int n )
{
        int i, j, k ;
        for ( i = n/2 ; i <= n ; i++ )
        {
                for ( j = 1 ; j <= n ; j = 2 * j )
                {
                        for ( k = 1 ; i <= n ; k = k*2 )
                                printf ( "Hello\n" ) ;
                }
        }
}
```

(n)
```
fun( int n )
{
        // Assume n >= 2
        int i, j, k ;
        while ( n > 1 )
                n = n /2 ;
}
```

(o)
```
fun( int n )
{
        int i, j ;
        for ( i = 1 ; i <= n ; i++ )
        {
                for ( j = 1 ; j <= n ; j = j + i )
                        printf ( "Hello\n" ) ;
        }
}
```

(p)
```
fun( )
{
        int i, j, n, k ;
        n = (2²)ᵏ ;
        for ( i = 1 ; i <= n ; i++ )
        {
                j = 2 ;
                while ( j <= n )
                {
                        j = j * j ;
                        printf ( "Hello\n" ) ;
                }
}
```

        }

[F] Arrange the following functions in ascending order of their growth
     rate:

        fun1 = 2^n
        fun2 = $n^{3/2}$
        fun3 = n log n
        fun4 = $n^{\log n}$

[G] Determine which of the following function is faster:

        $f(n) = n^3$ for $0 < n < 10000$
            $= n^2$ for $n >= 10000$

        $g(n) = n$ for $0 < n < 100$
            = n3 for $n > 100$

Coding Interview Questions

Exercise Level III

For each of the following pairs of functions f(n) and g(n), either f(n) =
O[g(n)] or g(n) = O[f(n)], but not both. Determine which the case is for
each of the following pairs:

(a) $f(n) = (n^2 - n)/2$, $g(n) = 6n$

(b) $f(n) = n + 2\sqrt{n}$, $g(n) = n^2$

(c) $f(n) = n + n \log n$, $g(n) = n\sqrt{n}$

(d) $f(n) = n^2 + 3n + 4$, $g(n) = n^3$

(e) $f(n) = n \log n$, $g(n) = n\sqrt{n} / 2$

(f) $f(n) = n + \log n$, $g(n) = \sqrt{n}$

(g) $f(n) = 2(\log n)^2$, $g(n) = \log n+1$

(h) $f(n) = 4n \log n+n$, $g(n) = (n^2-n)/2$

Case Scenario Exercise

Growth rates

List the following functions from highest to lowest order. If any are of the same order, circle them on your list.

2^n	$\log \log n$	$n^3 + \log n$	$\log n$	$n^2 + 5n^3$
2^{n-1}	n^2	n^3	$n \log n$	$(\log n)^2$
$\sqrt{n}$	6	$n!$	n	$(3/2)^n$

02

Chapter

Arrays

Friends Are Friends

Why This Chapter Matters?

Array is one data structure that has been used more than any other. Arrays are simple yet reliable and are used in more situations than you can count. Yet they have problems that are typical to them, which at times lead to serious performance issues. They are like old friends. You accept and live with their qualities—good as well as bad.

ata Structure is a way of organizing data in such a way that we can perform operations on the data in an effective way. Same data can be stored in different data structures. Each data structure has its own benefits and limitations. A data structure is not related with any specific language. All data structures can be implemented through languages like C, C++, Java, C#, Python, etc. In this book we would be using C language to implement various data structures.

Data structures are classified into two categories—linear and nonlinear. The elements in a linear data structure form a sequence, whereas elements in a nonlinear data structure do not.

There are two ways of representing linear data structures in memory— Array based lists (simply called arrays) and Linked Lists. In array the linear relationship between elements is established by storing its elements in sequential memory locations. In linked list the linear relationship is established through pointers or links. In a linked list each node contains the data and the address of the next node. Figure 2-1(a) and Figure 2-1(b) show the representation of an array and a linked list.

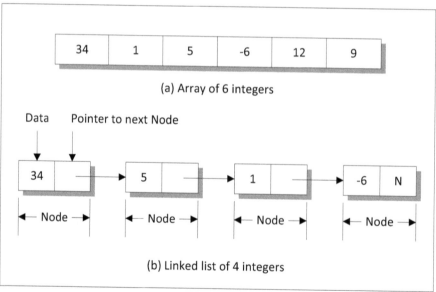

(a) Array of 6 integers

(b) Linked list of 4 integers

Figure 2-1. Array and Linked list.

Arrays are useful when the number of elements to be stored is fixed. They are easy to traverse, search and sort. On the other hand, linked lists are useful when number of data items in the collection is likely to vary. Linked lists are difficult to maintain as compared to an array. We would discuss linked lists in more detail in Chapter 3.

Arrays

An Array is a finite collection of similar elements stored in adjacent memory locations. An array containing **n** number of elements is referenced using an index that varies from **0** to **n - 1**. For example, the elements of an array **arr[n]** containing **n** elements are denoted by **arr[0]**, **arr[1], arr[2], ..., arr[n-1]**, where **0** is the lower bound of the array, **n - 1** is the upper bound and of the array and 0, 1, 2, etc. are indices of the array. A sample arrangement of array elements is shown in Figure 2-2.

a[0]	a[1]	a[2]	a[3]	a[4]	a[5]
34	1	5	-6	12	9

Figure 2-2. *Elements in an array with their indices.*

There are several operations that can be performed on an array. These operations are listed in Table 2-1.

Operation	Description
Traversal	Processing each element in the array
Search	Finding the location of an element with a given value
Insertion	Adding a new element to an array
Deletion	Removing an element from an array
Sorting	Organizing the array elements in some order
Merging	Combining two arrays into a single array
Reversing	Reversing the elements of an array

Table 2-1. *Operations performed on arrays.*

Let us now see a program that shows how to perform these operations on an array.

Honest Solid Code

{C++}

Program 2-1. Implementation of various array operations

```cpp
#include <iostream>
using namespace std ;
const int MAX = 5 ;

class array
{
    private :
        int arr[ MAX ] ;
    public :
        void insert ( int pos, int num ) ;
        void del ( int pos ) ;
        void reverse( ) ;
        void display( ) ;
        void search ( int num ) ;
} ;

// inserts an element num at given position pos
void array :: insert ( int pos, int num )
{
    int i ;
    // shift elements to right
    for ( i = MAX - 1 ; i >= pos ; i-- )
        arr[ i ] = arr[ i - 1 ] ;
    arr[ i ] = num ;
}

// deletes an element from the given position pos
void array :: del ( int pos )
{
    int i ;
    // skip to the desired position
    for ( i = pos ; i < MAX ; i++ )
        arr[ i - 1 ] = arr[ i ] ;
    arr[ i - 1 ] = 0 ;
}
```

```
// reverses the entire array
void array :: reverse( )
{
    for ( int  i = 0 ; i < MAX / 2 ; i++ )
    {
        int temp = arr[ i ] ;
        arr[ i ] = arr[ MAX - 1 - i ] ;
        arr[ MAX - 1 - i ] = temp ;
    }
}

// searches array for a given element num
void array :: search ( int num )
{
    int i ;
    for ( i = 0 ; i < MAX ; i++ )
    {
        if ( arr[ i ] == num )
        {
            cout << endl << "Element " << num
                << " is at " << ( i + 1) << "th position" ;
            return ;
        }
    }

    if ( i == MAX )
        cout << endl << "Element " << num << " is absent" ;
}

// displays the contents of an array
void array :: display( )
{
    cout << endl ;
    for ( int i = 0 ; i < MAX ; i++ )
        cout << arr[ i ] << " " ;
}

int main( )
{
    array a ;
    a.insert ( 1,11 ) ;
```

```
      a.insert ( 2,12 ) ;
      a.insert ( 3,13 ) ;
      a.insert ( 4,14 ) ;
      a.insert ( 5,15 ) ;
      cout << endl << "Elements of Array: " ;
      a.display( ) ;
      a.del ( 5 ) ;
      a.del ( 2 ) ;
      cout << endl << "After deletion: " ;
      a.display( ) ;
      a.insert ( 2, 222 ) ;
      a.insert ( 5, 555 ) ;
      cout << endl << "After insertion: " ;
      a.display( ) ;
      a.reverse( ) ;
      cout << endl << "After reversing: " ;
      a.display( ) ;
      a.search ( 222 ) ;
      a.search ( 666 ) ;
      return 0 ;
}
```

Output:

```
Elements of Array:
11    12    13    14    15
After deletion:
11    13    14    0    0
After insertion:
11    222    13    14    555
After reversing:
555    14    13    222    11
Element 222 is at 4th position
Element 666 is absent
```

In this program we have designed a class called **array**. It contains an array **arr** of 5 ints. The functions like **insert( )**, **del( )**, **display( )**, **reverse( )** and **search( )** access and manipulate the array **arr**.

The **insert( )** function takes two arguments, the position **pos** at which the new number has to be inserted and the number **num** that has to be inserted. In this function, firstly through a loop, we have shifted the numbers from the specified position, one place to the right of their existing position. Then we have placed the number **num** at position **pos**.

The **del( )** function deletes the element present at the given position **pos**. For this we have shifted the numbers placed after the position from where the number is to be deleted, one place to the left of their existing positions. The number at position **pos** is then overwritten with 0.

In **reverse( )** function we have reversed the entire array by swapping the elements **arr[0]** with **arr[4]**, **arr[1]** with **arr[3]** and so on. Note that swapping should continue for **MAX / 2** times only, irrespective of whether **MAX** is odd or even.

The **search( )** function searches the array for the specified number. For this the comparison is carried out until either the list is exhausted or a match is found. If the match is not found then the function displays the relevant message.

In the **display( )** function, the entire array is traversed to display the elements of the array.

Two-Dimensional Arrays

A 2-dimensional array is a collection of elements placed in **m** rows and **n** columns. The syntax used to declare a 2-D array includes two subscripts, of which one specifies the number of rows and the other specifies the number of columns of an array. These two subscripts are used to reference an element in an array. For example, **arr[3][4]** is a 2-D array containing 3 rows and 4 columns and **arr[0][2]** is an element placed at 0th row and 2nd column in the array. The two-dimensional array is also called a **matrix**. The pictorial representation of a matrix is shown in Figure 2-3.

		COLUMN			
		0	1	2	3
	0	12	1	-9	23
ROW	1	14	7	11	121
	2	6	78	15	34

Figure 2-3. Representation of a 2-D array.

Row Major and Column Major Arrangement

Rows and columns of a matrix are only a matter of imagination. When a matrix gets stored in memory all its elements are stored linearly since computer's memory can only be viewed as consecutive units of memory locations. This leads to two possible arrangements of elements in memory—Row Major Arrangement and Column Major Arrangement. Figure 2-4 illustrates these two possible arrangements for a 2-D array.

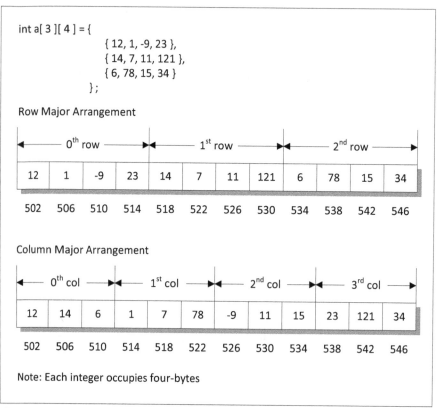

Figure 2-4. *Possible arrangements of 2-D array.*

Since the array elements are stored in adjacent memory locations we can access any element of the array once we know the base address (starting address) of the array and number of rows and columns present in the array.

For example, if the base address of the array shown in Figure 2-4 is 502 and we wish to refer the element 121, then the calculation involved would be as follows:

Row Major Arrangement

Element 121 is present at **a[1][3]**. Hence location of 121 would be

= 502 + 1 * 4 + 3 = 502 + 7 = 530

In general, for an array **a[m][n]** the address of element **a[i][j]** would be **Base address + i * n + j**.

Column Major Arrangement

Element 121 is present at **a[1][3]**. Hence location of 121 would be

= 502 + 3 * 3 + 1 = 502 + 10 = 542

In general for an array **a[m][n]** the address of element **a[i][j]** would be **Base address + j * m + i**. Note that C language permits only Row Major Arrangement.

Common Matrix Operations

Common matrix operations are addition, multiplication and transposition. The following program demonstrates these different matrix operations.

Honest Solid Code   {C++}

Program 2-2. Implementation of common matrix operations

```cpp
#include <iostream>
using namespace std ;
const int MAX = 3 ;

class matrix
{
    private :
        int mat[ MAX ][ MAX ] ;
    public :
        matrix( ) ;
        void create( ) ;
        void display( ) ;
        void matadd ( matrix &m1, matrix &m2 ) ;
        void matmul ( matrix &m1, matrix &m2 ) ;
        void transpose ( matrix &m1 ) ;
} ;
```

```
// initializes the matrix mat with 0
matrix :: matrix( )
{
    for ( int i = 0 ; i < MAX ; i++ )
    {
        for ( int j = 0 ; j < MAX ; j++ )
            mat[ i ][ j ] = 0 ;
    }
}

// creates matrix mat
void matrix :: create( )
{
    int n ;
    for ( int i = 0 ; i < MAX ; i++ )
    {
        for ( int j = 0 ; j < MAX ; j++ )
        {
            cout << endl << "Enter the element: " ;
            cin >> n ;
            mat[ i ][ j ] = n ;
        }
    }
}

// displays the contents of matrix
void matrix :: display( )
{
    for ( int i = 0 ; i < MAX ; i++ )
    {
        for ( int j = 0 ; j < MAX ; j++ )
            cout << mat[ i ][ j ] << " " ;
        cout << endl ;
    }
}

// adds two matrices m1 and m2
void matrix :: matadd ( matrix &m1, matrix &m2 )
{
    for ( int i = 0 ; i < MAX ; i++ )
```

```
    {
        for ( int j = 0 ; j < MAX ; j++ )
            mat[ i ][ j ] = m1.mat[ i ][ j ] + m2.mat[ i ][ j ] ;
    }
}

// multiplies two matrices m1 and m2
void matrix :: matmul ( matrix &m1, matrix &m2 )
{
    for ( int k = 0 ; k < MAX ; k++ )
    {
        for ( int i = 0 ; i < MAX ; i++ )
        {
            for ( int j = 0 ; j < MAX ; j++ )
                mat[ k ][ i ] += m1.mat[ k ][ j ] * m2.mat[ j ][ i ] ;
        }
    }
}

// obtains transpose of matrix m1
void matrix :: transpose ( matrix &m1 )
{
    for ( int i = 0 ; i < MAX ; i++ )
    {
        for ( int j = 0 ; j < MAX ; j++ )
            mat[ i ][ j ] = m1.mat[ j ][ i ] ;
    }
}

int main( )
{
    matrix mat1 ;
    cout << endl << "Enter elements for first array:" << endl ;
    mat1.create( ) ;

    matrix mat2 ;
    cout << endl << "Enter elements for second array:" << endl ;
    mat2.create( ) ;

    cout << endl << "First Array:" << endl ;
    mat1.display( ) ;
```

```
        cout << endl << "Second Array:" << endl ;
        mat2.display( ) ;

        matrix mat3 ;
        mat3.matadd ( mat1, mat2 ) ;
        cout << endl << "After Addition:" << endl ;
        mat3.display( ) ;

        matrix mat4 ;
        mat4.matmul ( mat1, mat2 ) ;
        cout << endl << "After Multiplication:" << endl ;
        mat4.display( ) ;

        matrix mat5 ;
        mat5.transpose ( mat1 ) ;
        cout << endl << "Transpose of first matrix:" << endl ;
        mat5.display( ) ;
        return 0 ;
}
```

Output:

Enter elements for first array:
Enter the element: 1
Enter the element: 2
Enter the element: 3
Enter the element: 2
Enter the element: 1
Enter the element: 4
Enter the element: 4
Enter the element: 3
Enter the element: 2

Enter elements for second array:
Enter the element: 3
Enter the element: 2
Enter the element: 3
Enter the element: 4
Enter the element: 3
Enter the element: 2
Enter the element: 1
Enter the element: 3

Enter the element: 1

First Array:
```
1    2    3
2    1    4
4    3    2
```
Second Array:
```
3    2    3
4    3    2
1    3    1
```
After Addition:
```
4    4    6
6    4    6
5    6    3
```
After Multiplication:
```
14    17    10
14    19    12
26    23    20
```
Transpose of first matrix:
```
1    2    4
2    1    3
3    4    2
```

In this program we have designed a class called **matrix**. This class contains functions that perform different matrix operations like addition, multiplication, transposition, etc. The **create( )** function creates a 2-D array containing 3 rows and 3 columns. The **display( )** function displays the elements of the matrix.

The function **matadd( )** adds the elements of two matrices **mat1.mat** and **mat2.mat**. The result is stored in matrix **mat** of the object **mat3**, that has called the **matadd( )** function. Similarly, the function **matmul( )** multiplies the elements of matrix **mat1.mat** with the elements of matrix **mat2.mat** and stores the result into the matrix **mat** of the object **mat4** that called the function.

The function **transpose( )**, transposes a matrix. A transpose of a matrix is obtained by interchanging the rows with corresponding columns of a given matrix. The transposed matrix is stored in matrix **mat** of the object **mat5**.

Multidimensional Arrays

A 3-dimensional array can be thought of as an array of arrays of arrays. Figure 2-5 shows a 3-D array, which is a collection of three 2-D arrays each containing 4 rows and 2 columns.

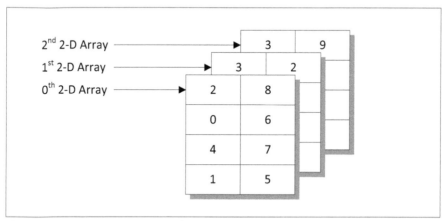

Figure 2-5. *Representation of a 3-D array.*

This array can be defined as:

int a[3][4][2] = {

           { { 2, 8 }, { 0, 6 }, { 4, 7 }, { 1, 5 } },
           { { 3, 2 }, { 8, 6 }, { 1, 6 }, { 4, 5 } },
           { { 3, 9 }, { 1, 8 }, { 6, 5 }, { 4, 0 } }

    };

The outer array has three elements, each of which is a 2D array, which in turn holds four 1D arrays containing two integers each. Note that the arrangement shown in Figure 2-5 is only conceptually true. In memory the same array elements are stored linearly as shown in Figure 2-6.

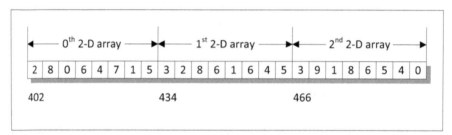

Figure 2-6. *Memory representation of a 3-D array.*

As stated earlier, C permits only a Row Major arrangement for multi-dimensional arrays. Let us determine the location of element 9 in the array shown in Figure 2-6. Element 9 is present at **a[2][0][1]** indicating that it is present in 0th row, 1st column of 2nd 2-D array. Hence address of 9 would be

$402 + 2 * 4 * 2 + 0 * 2 + 1 = 402 + 17 = 470$

For any 3-D array **a[x][y][z]** arranged in Row Major fashion the element **a[i][j][k]** can be accessed using **Base address + i * y * z + j * z + k.**

The formula for Column Major arrangement would be **Base address + i * y * z + k * y + j.**

On similar lines for a 4-D array **a[w][x][y][z]** the element **a[i][j][k][l]** can be accessed using following formulae:

Row Major : **Base address + i * x * y * z + j * y * z + k * z + l**

Column Major : **Base address + i * x * y * z + j * y * z + l * y + k**

Arrays and Polynomials

Polynomials like $5X^4 + 2X^3 + 7X^2 + 10X - 8$ can be maintained using an array. The simplest way to represent a polynomial of degree "n" is to store the coefficient of (n + 1) terms of a polynomial in an array. For this each element of the array should consist of two values—coefficient and exponent. While storing the polynomial it is assumed that the exponent of each successive term is less than that of the previous term. Once we build an array to represent a polynomial, we can use it to perform common polynomial operations like addition and multiplication. The following program demonstrates how we can store polynomials and add them.

| Honest Solid Code | {C++} |

Program 2-3. Implementation of polynomial addition

```
#include <iostream>
using namespace std ;
const int MAX = 10 ;

class poly
{
    private :
        struct term
```

```
        {
            int coeff ;
            int exp ;
        } t[ MAX ] ;
        int noofterms ;

public :
        poly( ) ;
        void polyappend ( int c, int e ) ;
        void polyadd ( poly &p1, poly &p2 ) ;
        void display( ) ;
} ;

// initializes data members of class poly
poly :: poly( )
{
    noofterms = 0 ;
    for ( int i = 0 ; i < MAX ; i++ )
    {
        t[ i ].coeff = 0 ;
        t[ i ].exp = 0 ;
    }
}

// adds the term of polynomial to the array t
void poly :: polyappend ( int c, int e )
{
    t[ noofterms ].coeff = c ;
    t[ noofterms ].exp =  e ;
    noofterms++ ;
}

// displays the polynomial equation
void poly :: display( )
{
    int flag = 0 ;
    for ( int i = 0 ; i < noofterms ; i++ )
    {
        if ( t[ i ].exp != 0 )
            cout << t[ i ].coeff << "x^" << t[ i ].exp << " + " ;
        else
```

```
            {
                cout << t[ i ].coeff ;
                flag = 1 ;
            }
        }
        if ( !flag )
            cout << "\b\b  " ;
}

// adds two polynomials p1 and p2
void poly :: polyadd ( poly& p1, poly& p2 )
{
    int c = p1.noofterms > p2.noofterms ? p1.noofterms : p2.noofterms ;

    for ( int i = 0, j = 0 ; i <= c ; noofterms++ )
    {
        if ( p1.t[ i ].coeff == 0 && p2.t[ j ].coeff == 0 )
            break ;
        if ( p1.t[ i ].exp >= p2.t[ j ].exp )
        {
            if ( p1.t[ i ].exp == p2.t[ j ].exp )
            {
                t[ noofterms ].coeff = p1.t[ i ].coeff + p2.t[ j ].coeff ;
                t[ noofterms ].exp = p1.t[ i ].exp ;
                i++ ;
                j++ ;
            }
            else
            {
                t[ noofterms ].coeff = p1.t[ i ].coeff ;
                t[ noofterms ].exp = p1.t[ i ].exp ;
                i++ ;
            }
        }
        else
        {
            t[ noofterms ].coeff = p2.t[ j ].coeff ;
            t[ noofterms ].exp = p2.t[ j ].exp ;
            j++ ;
        }
    }
```

```
}

int main( )
{
    poly p1 ;

    p1.polyappend ( 1, 7 ) ;
    p1.polyappend ( 2, 6 ) ;
    p1.polyappend ( 3, 5 ) ;
    p1.polyappend ( 4, 4 ) ;
    p1.polyappend ( 5, 2 ) ;

    poly p2 ;
    p2.polyappend ( 1, 4 ) ;
    p2.polyappend ( 1, 3 ) ;
    p2.polyappend ( 1, 2 ) ;
    p2.polyappend ( 1, 1 ) ;
    p2.polyappend ( 2, 0 ) ;

    poly p3 ;
    p3.polyadd ( p1, p2 ) ;

    cout << endl << "First polynomial:" << endl ;
    p1.display( ) ;

    cout << endl << "Second polynomial:" << endl ;
    p2.display( ) ;

    cout << endl << "Resultant polynomial:" << endl ;
    p3.display( ) ;

    return 0 ;
}
```

Output:

First polynomial:
1x^7 + 2x^6 + 3x^5 + 4x^4 + 5x^2
Second polynomial:
1x^4 + 1x^3 + 1x^2 + 1x^1 + 2
Resultant polynomial:

1x^7 + 2x^6 + 3x^5 + 5x^4 + 1x^3 + 6x^2 + 1x^1 + 2

In this program, the class **poly** contains a structure called **term**. This structure stores the coefficient and exponent of the term of a polynomial. The data member **noofterms** stores the total number of terms that an object of **poly** class is supposed to hold. The function **polyappend( )** adds the term of a polynomial to the array **t**. The function **polyadd( )** adds the polynomials represented by the two objects **p1** and **p2**. The function **display( )** displays the polynomial.

In **main( )**, we have called the function **polyappend( )** several times to build the two polynomials which are represented by the objects **p1** and **p2**. Next, the function **polyadd( )** is called through the object **p3** to carry out the addition of two polynomials. In this function, arrays representing the two polynomials are traversed. While traversing, the polynomials are compared on a term-by-term basis. If the exponents of the two terms being compared are equal then their coefficients are added and the result is stored in the third polynomial. If the exponents of two terms are not equal then the term with the bigger exponent is added to the third polynomial. If the term with an exponent is present in one of the objects of **poly**, then that term is added as it is to the third polynomial.

Lastly, the terms of the resulting polynomial are displayed using the function **display( )**.

Multiplication of Polynomials

Let us now see a program that carries out multiplication of two polynomials.

Honest Solid Code　　　　　　　　　　　{C++}

Program 2-4. Implementation of polynomial multiplication

```cpp
#include <iostream>
using namespace std ;
const int MAX = 10 ;

class poly
{
    private :
```

```
        struct term
        {
            int coeff ;
            int exp ;
        } t[ MAX ] ;
        int noofterms ;

    public :
        poly( ) ;
        void polyappend ( int c, int e ) ;
        void polyadd ( poly &p1, poly &p2 ) ;
        void polymul ( poly &p1, poly &p2 ) ;
        void display( ) ;
} ;

// initializes data members of class poly
poly :: poly( )
{
    noofterms = 0 ;
    for ( int i = 0 ; i < MAX ; i++ )
    {
        t[ i ].coeff = 0 ;
        t[ i ].exp = 0 ;
    }
}

// adds the term of polynomial to the array t
void poly :: polyappend ( int c, int e )
{
    t[ noofterms ].coeff = c ;
    t[ noofterms ].exp = e ;
    noofterms++ ;
}

// displays the polynomial equation
void poly :: display( )
{
    int flag = 0 ;
    for ( int i = 0 ; i < noofterms ; i++ )
    {
        if ( t[ i ].exp != 0 )
```

```
                cout << t[ i ].coeff << "x^" << t[ i ].exp << " + " ;
        else
        {
            cout << t[ i ].coeff ;
            flag = 1 ;
        }
    }
    if ( !flag )
        cout << "\b\b " ;
}

// add two polynomials p1 and p2
void poly :: polyadd ( poly &p1, poly &p2 )
{
    int coeff, exp ;
    poly p ;

    int c = p1.noofterms ;
    int d = p2.noofterms ;

    for ( int i = 0, j = 0 ; i <= c || j <= d ; )
    {
        if ( p1.t[ i ].coeff == 0 && p2.t[ j ].coeff == 0 )
            break ;
        if ( p1.t[ i ].exp >= p2.t[ j ].exp )
        {
            if ( p1.t[ i ].exp == p2.t[ j ].exp )
            {
                coeff = p1.t[ i ].coeff + p2.t[ j ].coeff ;
                exp = p1.t[ i ].exp ;
                i++ ;
                j++ ;
            }
            else
            {
                coeff = p1.t[ i ].coeff ;
                exp = p1.t[ i ].exp ;
                i++ ;
            }
        }
        else
```

```
        {
            coeff = p2.t[ j ].coeff ;
            exp = p2.t[ j ].exp ;
            j++ ;
        }
        p.polyappend ( coeff, exp ) ;
    }
    *this = p ;
}

// multiply two polynomials p1 and p2
void poly :: polymul ( poly &p1, poly &p2 )
{
    int coeff, exp ;
    poly t1, t2 ;

    if ( p1.noofterms != 0 && p2.noofterms != 0 )
    {
        for ( int i = 0 ; i < p1.noofterms ; i++ )
        {
            poly p ;
            for ( int j = 0 ; j < p2.noofterms ; j++ )
            {
                coeff = p1.t[ i ].coeff * p2.t[ j ].coeff ;
                exp = p1.t[ i ].exp + p2.t[ j ].exp ;
                p.polyappend ( coeff, exp ) ;
            }

            if ( i != 0 )
            {
                t2.polyadd ( t1, p ) ;
                t1 = t2 ;
            }
            else
                t1 = p ;
        }
        *this = t2 ;
    }
}

int main( )
```

```
{
    poly p1 ;
    p1.polyappend ( 1, 4 ) ;
    p1.polyappend ( 2, 3 ) ;
    p1.polyappend ( 2, 2 ) ;
    p1.polyappend ( 2, 1 ) ;

    poly p2 ;
    p2.polyappend ( 2, 3 ) ;
    p2.polyappend ( 3, 2 ) ;
    p2.polyappend ( 4, 1 ) ;

    poly p3 ;
    p3.polymul( p1, p2 ) ;

    cout << endl << "First polynomial: " << endl ;
    p1.display( ) ;
    cout << endl << "Second polynomial: " << endl ;
    p2.display( ) ;
    cout << endl << "Resultant polynomial: " << endl ;
    p3.display( ) ;

    return 0 ;
}
```

Output:

First polynomial:
$1x^4 + 2x^3 + 2x^2 + 2x^1$
Second polynomial:
$2x^3 + 3x^2 + 4x^1$
Resultant polynomial:
$2x^7 + 7x^6 + 14x^5 + 18x^4 + 14x^3 + 8x^2$

To carry out multiplication of two given polynomial equations, the **poly** class contains one more function **polymul( )**. As done in previous program, here too we have called **polyappend( )** function several times to build the two polynomials which are represented by the objects **p1** and **p2**. Next the function **polymul( )** is called through the object **p3** to carry out the multiplication of two polynomials.

In **polymul( )** function, first we have checked if the two objects **p1** and **p2** are non-empty. If they are not, then the control goes in a pair of **for** loops. Here each term of first polynomial contained in **p1** is multiplied with every term of second polynomial contained in **p2**. While doing so, we have called **polyappend( )** to add the terms to **p**. The first resultant polynomial equation is stored in temporary object **t1** of **poly** class. There onwards the function **polyadd( )** is called to add the resulting polynomial equations.

Lastly, the terms of the resulting polynomial are displayed using the function **display( )**.

Chapter Bullets

Summary of chapter

(a) Array is a collection of similar elements stored in adjacent memory locations.

(b) Arrays cannot grow or shrink dynamically. Hence they are useful in situations where number of elements stored in it is fixed.

(c) Common array operations include traversal, searching, sorting, insertion, deletion, merging and reversal.

(d) Two-dimensional arrays can be arranged in memory either in row-major or column-major fashion.

(e) All matrix operations like transpose, addition, multiplication can be implemented using two-dimensional arrays.

(f) Array of structures can be used to store a polynomial and to perform polynomial operations like addition and multiplication.

Check Your Progress

Exercise - Level I

[A] Fill in the blanks:

(a) A data structure is said to be _____ if its elements form a sequence.

(b) An Array is a collection of _____ elements stored in _____ memory locations.

(c) Index of an array containing **n** elements varies from _____ to _____.

(d) A 2-D array is also called _____.

[B] Pick up the correct alternative for each of the following questions:

(a) To traverse an array means
(1) To process each element in an array
(2) To delete an element from an array
(3) To insert an element into an array
(4) To combine two arrays into a single array

(b) A program P reads in 500 integers in the range [0..100] representing the scores of 500 students. It then prints the frequency of each score above 50. What would be the best way for P to store the frequencies?
(1) An array of 50 numbers
(2) An array of 100 numbers
(3) An array of 500 numbers
(4) A dynamically allocated array of 550 numbers

(c) Which of the following operations is not O(1) for an array of sorted data. You may assume that array elements are distinct.
(1) Find the ith largest element
(2) Delete an element
(3) Find the ith smallest element
(4) All of the above

Sharpen Your Skills

Exercise - Level II

[C] Answer the following:

(a) Find the location of the element **a[1][2][2][1]** from a 4-D integer array **a[4][3][4][3]** if the base address of the array is **1002**.

(b) Design a data structure for a banking system where the maximum number of clients is 150. Information to be stored about clients— name, address, account no., balance, status as Low/Medium/High depending on balance.

(c) Design a data structure for Income Tax department to hold information for maximum 200 persons. Information to be stored about persons—Income Tax no., tax amount, name, address, whether tax paid or not for previous year, group as High/Low depending on amount of tax to be paid and category which would vary from 1 to 10.

[D] Write programs for the following:

(a) Write a program to find out the maximum and the second maximum number from an array of integers.

(b) Build an array called **chess** to represent a chessboard and write a function that would be capable of displaying position of each coin on the chessboard.

(c) There are two arrays **A** and **B**. **A** contains 25 elements, whereas, **B** contains 30 elements. Write a function to create an array **C** that contains only those elements that are common to **A** and **B**.

Coding Interview Questions

Exercise Level III

(a) The Mode of an array of numbers is the number **m** in the array that is repeated most frequently. If more than one number is repeated with equal maximal frequencies, there is no mode. Write a program that accepts an array of numbers and returns the mode or an indication that the mode does not exist.

(b) Write a program to delete duplicate elements from an array of 20 integers.

(c) A square matrix is symmetric if for all values of **i** and **j** a[i][j] = a[j][i]. Write a program, which verifies whether a given 5 x 5 matrix is symmetric, or not.

Case Scenario Exercise

Orthogonal Matrix

A square matrix is said to be Orthogonal if the matrix obtained by multiplying the matrix with its transpose is an identity matrix. In other words, if A is a matrix and T is its transpose, then matrix B obtained by multiplying A with T is called orthogonal if it is an identity matrix. An identity matrix is a square matrix in which the elements in the leading diagonal are 1. Write a program that receives a square matrix and determines whether it is Orthogonal or not.

Orthogonal matrices have applications in field of numerical linear algebra.

Case Scenario Exercise

Longest increasing sub-sequence

One of the interesting problems in Computer Science is to find the longest increasing subsequence in a given sequence. The subsequence should be as long as possible and its elements must be in ascending order. The subsequence elements need not be in adjacent locations and the elements need not be unique.

For example, in the following sequence

0, 8, 4, 12, 2, 10, 6, 14, 1, 9, 5, 13, 3, 11, 7, 15

the longest increasing subsequence is

0, 2, 6, 9, 11, 15.

This subsequence has length six; the input sequence has no seven-member increasing subsequences. The longest increasing subsequence in this example is not unique. 0, 4, 6, 9, 11, 15 or 0, 4, 6, 9, 13, 15 are other increasing subsequences of equal length in the same input sequence.

Write a program to obtain the longest increasing subsequence in a given sequence.

Longest increasing subsequences have applications in fields of random matrix theory, representation theory, and physics.

03
Chapter

—

Linked Lists

Stay connected

Why This Chapter Matters?

United we stand, divided we fall! More united and
connected we are, more is the flexibility and
scalability. Same is true with linked lists. Linked lists
are used at numerous places in Computer Science.
The flexibility and performance they offer is worth
the pain of learning them.

For storing similar data in memory we can use either an array or a linked list. Arrays are simple to understand and elements of an array are easily accessible. But arrays suffer from the following limitations:

—   Arrays have a fixed dimension. Once the size of an array is decided it cannot be increased or decreased during execution.

—   Insertion of a new element in an array is tedious because during insertion each element after the specified position has to be shifted one position to the right.

—   Deletion of an existing element in an array is inefficient because during deletion each element after the specified position has to be shifted one position to the left.

Linked list overcomes all these disadvantages. A linked list can grow and shrink in size during its lifetime. Thus, there is no maximum size of a linked list. Also, unlike arrays, while inserting or deleting elements in a linked list shifting of existing elements is not required.

What is a Linked List

While the elements of an array occupy contiguous memory locations, those of a linked list are not constrained to be stored in adjacent locations. The order of the elements is maintained by explicit links between them. For instance, the marks obtained by different students can be stored in a linked list as shown in Figure 3-1.

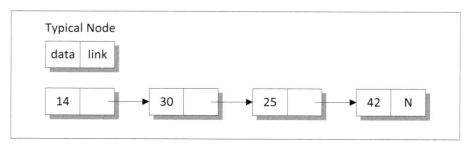

Figure 3-1. *Linked list.*

Observe that the linked list is a collection of elements called nodes, each of which stores two items of information—an element of the list and a link. In Figure 3-1, the **data** part of each node consists of the marks obtained by a student and the **link** part contains address of the next node. Thus the **link** part is a pointer to the next node. Hence it is shown using an arrow. The **NULL** (N) in the last node indicates that it is the last node in the list.

Operations on Linked List

Several operations can be performed on linked lists. This includes building a linked list by adding new node (at the beginning, at the end or in the middle of the linked list), deleting a node, display contents of all nodes, etc. The following program shows how to implement these operations. Go through the program carefully, a step at a time to understand the working of these operations.

Honest Solid Code   {C++}

Program 3-1. Implementation of various linked list operations

```cpp
#include <iostream>
using namespace std ;

class linklist
{
    private :
        // structure containing a data part and link part
        struct node
        {
            int data ;
            node * link ;
        } *p ;

    public :
        linklist( ) ;
        void append ( int num ) ;
        void addatbeg ( int num ) ;
        void addafter ( int loc, int num ) ;
        void display( ) ;
        int count( ) ;
        void del ( int num ) ;
        ~linklist( ) ;
} ;

// initializes data member
linklist :: linklist( )
{
```

```
        p = NULL ;
}

// adds a node at the end of a linked list
void linklist :: append ( int num )
{
    node *temp, *r ;

    // if the list is empty, create first node
    if ( p == NULL )
    {
        temp = new node ;
        temp -> data = num ;
        temp -> link = NULL ;
        p = temp ;
    }
    else
    {
        // go to last node
        temp = p ;
        while ( temp -> link != NULL )
            temp = temp -> link ;

        // add node at the end
        r = new node ;
        r -> data = num ;
        r -> link = NULL ;
        temp -> link = r ;
    }
}

// adds a new node at the beginning of the linked list
void linklist :: addatbeg ( int num )
{
    node *temp ;

    // add new node
    temp = new node ;
    temp -> data = num ;
    temp -> link = p ;
    p = temp ;
```

```
}

// adds a new node after the specified number of nodes
void linklist :: addafter ( int loc, int num )
{
    node *temp, *r ;
    temp = p ;

    // skip to desired portion
    for ( int i = 0 ; i < loc - 1 ; i++ )
    {
        temp = temp -> link ;
        // if end of linked list is encountered
        if ( temp == NULL )
        {
            cout << "\nThere are less than " << loc
                << " elements in list" << endl ;
            return ;
        }
    }

    // insert new node
    r = new node ;
    r -> data = num ;
    r -> link = temp -> link ;
    temp -> link = r ;
}

// displays the contents of the linked list
void linklist :: display( )
{
    node *temp = p ;
    // traverse the entire linked list
    while ( temp != NULL )
    {
        cout << temp -> data << " " ;
        temp = temp -> link ;
    }
    cout << endl ;
}
```

```
// counts the number of nodes present in the linked list
int linklist :: count( )
{
    int c = 0 ;
    node *temp = p ;
    // traverse the entire linked list
    while ( temp != NULL )
    {
        temp = temp -> link ;
        c++ ;
    }
    return c ;
}

// deletes the specified node from the linked list
void linklist :: del ( int num )
{
    node *old, *temp ;
    temp = p ;
    while ( temp != NULL )
    {
        if ( temp -> data == num )
        {
            // if node to be deleted is the
            // first node in the linked list
            if ( temp == p )
                p = temp -> link ;

            // delete the intermediate nodes in the linked list
            else
                old -> link = temp -> link ;

            // free the memory occupied by the node
            delete temp ;
            return ;
        }
        // traverse the linked list till the last node is reached
        else
        {
            // old points to the previous node
            old = temp ;
```

```
            // go to the next node
            temp = temp -> link ;
        }
    }
    cout << "Element " << num << " not found" << endl ;
}

// deallocates memory
linklist :: ~linklist( )
{
    node *q ;
    while ( p != NULL )
    {
        q = p -> link ;
        delete p ;
        p = q  ;
    }
}

int main( )
{
    linklist l ;
    cout << "No. of elements: " << l.count( ) << endl ;
    l.append ( 14 ) ; l.append ( 30 ) ; l.append ( 25 ) ;
    l.append ( 42 ) ; l.append ( 17 ) ;
    cout << "Elements in the linked list: " ;
    l.display( ) ;
    l.addatbeg ( 99 ) ; l.addatbeg ( 88 ) ; l.addatbeg ( 77 ) ;
    cout << "Linked list after addition at the beginning: " << endl ;
    l.display( ) ;
    l.addafter ( 3, 41 ) ; l.addafter ( 6, 89 ) ; l.addafter ( 10, 60 ) ;
    cout << "Linked list after addition at given position: " << endl ;
    l.display( ) ;
    cout << "No. of elements: " << l.count( ) ;
    l.del ( 99 ) ; l.del ( 42 ) ; l.del ( 10 ) ;
    cout << "Linked list after deletion: " << endl ;
    l.display( ) ;
    cout << "No. of elements: " << l.count( ) ;
    return 0 ;
}
```

Output:

No. of elements: 0
Elements in the linked list: 14 30 25 42 17
Linked list after addition at the beginning:
77 88 99 14 30 25 42 17
Linked list after addition at given position:
77 88 99 41 14 30 89 25 42 17 60
No. of elements: 11Element 10 not found
Linked list after deletion:
77 88 41 14 30 89 25 17 60
No. of elements: 9

To begin with we have designed a class **linklist**, which contains a structure to represent a node. The structure **node** contains a data part and a link part. The variable **p** has been declared as pointer to a node. We have used this pointer as pointer to the first node in the linked list. No matter how many nodes get added to the linked list, **p** would continue to point to the first node in the list. When no node has been added to the list, **p** has been set to **NULL** to indicate that the list is empty.

The **append( )** function has to deal with two situations:

(a) The node is being added to an empty list.
(b) The node is being added at the end of an existing list.

In the first case, the condition

if (p == NULL)

gets satisfied. Hence, memory is allocated for the node using **new** operator. The **data** and the **link** part of this node are set up using the statements

temp -> data = num ;
temp -> link = NULL ;

Lastly, **p** is made to point to this node, since the first node has been added to the list and **p** must always point to the first node.

In the other case, when the linked list is not empty, the condition
if (p == NULL)

would fail, since **p** is non-**NULL**. Now **temp** is made to point to the first node in the list through the statement

temp = p ;

Then using **temp** we have traversed through the entire linked list using the statements

while (temp -> link != NULL)
   temp = temp -> link ;

The position of the pointers before and after traversing the linked list is shown in Figure 3-2.

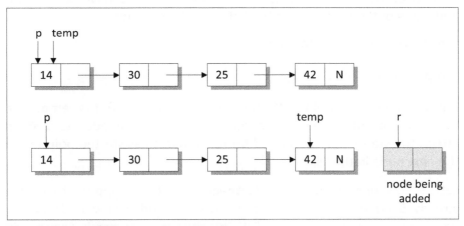

Figure 3-2. *Working of **append( )** function.*

Each time through the loop the statement **temp = temp -> link** makes **temp** point to the next node in the list. When **temp** reaches the last node the condition **temp -> link != NULL** would fail. Once outside the loop we allocate memory for the new node through the statement

r =new node ;

Then this new node's **data** part is set with **num** and **link** part with **NULL**. Note that this node is now going to be the last node in the list.

All that now remains to be done is connecting the previous last node with the new last node. The previous last node is being pointed to by **temp** and the new last node is being pointed to by **r**. They are connected through the statement

temp -> link = r ;

There is often confusion as to how the statement **temp = temp -> link** makes **temp** point to the next node in the list. Let us understand this with the help of an example. Suppose in a linked list containing 4 nodes, **temp** is pointing at the first node. This is shown in Figure 4-3.

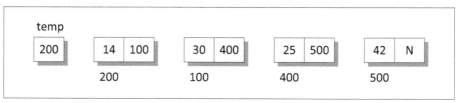

Figure 3-3. Connection of nodes.

Instead of showing the links to the next node we have shown the addresses of the next node in the link part of each node.

When we execute the statement

temp = temp -> link ;

the right hand side yields **100**. This address is now stored in **temp**. As a result, **temp** starts pointing to the node present at address **100**. In effect, the statement has shifted **temp** so that it has started pointing to the next node in the list.

Let us now understand the **addatbeg( )** function. Suppose there are already 5 nodes in the list and we wish to add a new node at the beginning of this existing linked list. This situation is shown in Figure 3-4.

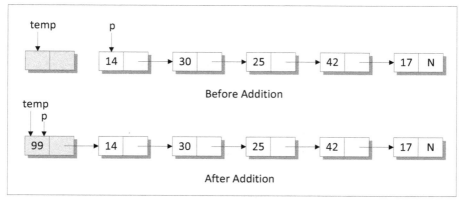

Figure 3-4. *Working of addatbeg( )* function.

For adding a new node at the beginning, firstly memory is allocated for this node and data is stored in it through the statement temp -> data = num ;

Now we need to make the **link** part of this node point to the existing first node. This has been achieved through the statement

temp -> link = p ;

Lastly, this new node must be made the first node in the list. This has been attained through the statement

p = temp ;

The **addafter( )** function permits us to add a new node after a specified number of node in the linked list. In this function, to begin with, through a loop we skip the desired number of nodes after which a new node is to be added. Suppose we wish to add a new node containing data as **41** after the 3rd node in the list. The position of pointers once the control reaches outside the **for** loop is shown in Figure 3-5(a). Now memory is allocated for the node to be inserted and **41** is stored in the **data** part of it.

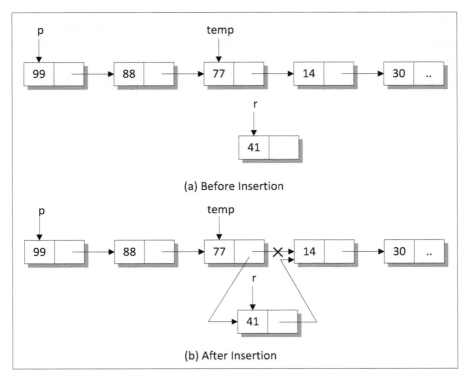

Figure 3-5. Working of *addafter( )* function.

All that remains to be done is readjustment of links such that **41** goes in between **77** and **14**. This is achieved through the statements

r -> link = temp -> link ;
temp -> link = r ;

The first statement makes **link** part of node containing **41** to point to the node containing **14**. The second statement ensures that the **link** part of node containing **77** points to the node containing **41**. On execution of the second statement the earlier link between **77** and **14** is severed. So now **77** no longer points to **14**, it points to **41**.

The **display( )** and **count( )** functions are straight forward. I will leave them for you to understand.

That brings us to the last function in the program i.e. **del( )**. In this function through the **while** loop, we have traversed through the entire linked list, checking at each node, whether it is the node to be deleted. If so, we have checked if the node being deleted is the first node in the linked list. If it is so, we have simply shifted **p** to the next node and then deleted the earlier node.

If the node to be deleted is an intermediate node, then the position of various pointers and links before and after the deletion is shown in Figure 3-6.

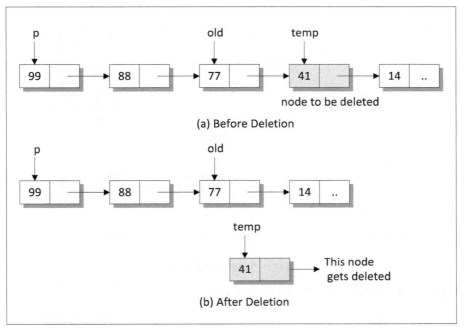

Figure 3-6. *Working of del( ) function.*

More Linked Lists

A common and a wrong impression that beginners carry is that a linked list is used only for storing integers. However, a linked list can virtually be used for storing any similar data. For example, there can be a linked list of **float**s, a linked list of names, or even a linked list of records, where each record contains name, age and salary of an employee. These linked lists are shown in Figure 3-7.

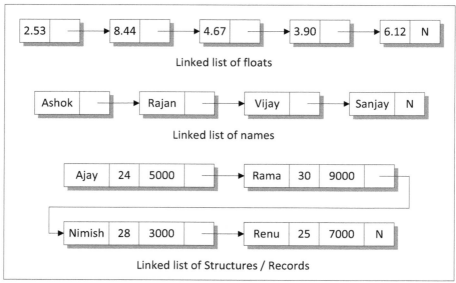

Figure 3-7. *Different types of linked list.*

Reversing the Links

Having had a feel of linked list, let us now explore some more operations that can be performed on a linked list. How about reversing the links in the existing linked list such that the last node becomes the first node and the first becomes the last? Here is a program that shows how this reversal of links can be achieved.

Honest Solid Code	{C++}

Program 3-2. Program to reverse a linked list

```cpp
#include <iostream>
using namespace std ;

class linklist
{
    private :
        // structure containing a data part and link part */
        struct node
        {
            int data ;
            node *link ;
        } *p;
```

```
    public :
        linklist( ) ;
        void addatbeg ( int num ) ;
        void reverse( ) ;
        void display( ) ;
        ~linklist( ) ;
} ;

// initializes data member
linklist :: linklist( )
{
    p = NULL ;
}

// adds a new node at the beginning of the linked list
void linklist :: addatbeg ( int num )
{
    node *temp ;
    // add new node
    temp = new node ;
    temp -> data = num ;
    temp -> link = p ;
    p = temp ;
}

// reverses the linked list
void linklist :: reverse( )
{
    node *q, *r, *s ;

    q = p ;
    r = NULL ;

    // traverse the entire linked list
    while ( q != NULL )
    {
        s = r ;
        r = q ;
        q = q -> link ;
        r -> link = s ;
```

```cpp
    }

    p = r ;
}

// displays the contents of the linked list
void linklist :: display( )
{
    node *temp = p ;
    // traverse the entire linked list
    while ( temp != NULL )
    {
        cout << temp -> data << " " ;
        temp = temp -> link ;
    }
    cout << endl ;
}

// deallocates memory
linklist :: ~linklist( )
{
    node *q ;
    while ( p != NULL )
    {
        q = p -> link ;
        delete p ;
        p = q ;
    }
}

int main( )
{
    linklist l ;

    l.addatbeg ( 7 ) ;
    l.addatbeg ( 43 ) ;
    l.addatbeg ( 17 ) ;
    l.addatbeg ( 3 ) ;
    l.addatbeg ( 23 ) ;
    l.addatbeg ( 5 ) ;
```

```
        cout << "Elements before reversing: " << endl ;
        l.display( ) ;
        l.reverse( ) ;
        cout << "Elements after reversing: " << endl ;
        l.display( ) ;
        return 0 ;
}
```

Output:

Elements before reversing:
5 23 3 17 43 7
Elements after reversing:
7 43 17 3 23 5

In the function **reverse( )** to traverse the linked list a variable **q** of the type **struct node *** is required. We have initialized **q** with **p**. So **q** also starts pointing to the first node.

To begin with, we need to store the **NULL** value in the **link** part of the first node, which is done through the statements

```
s = r ;
r = q ;
r -> link = s ;
```

r which is of the type **struct node *** is initialized to a **NULL** value. Since **r** contains **NULL**, **s** would also contain **NULL**. Now **r** is assigned **q** so that **r** also starts pointing to the first node. Finally **r -> link** is assigned **s** so that **r -> link** becomes **NULL**, which is nothing but the **link** part of the first node.

But if we store a **NULL** value in the **link** part of the first node then the address of the second node will be lost. Hence, before storing a **NULL** value in the **link** part of the first node, **q** is made to point to the second node through the statement

```
q = q -> link ;
```

During the second iteration of the **while** loop, **r** points to the first node and **q** points to the second node. Now the **link** part of the second node should point to the first node. This is done through the same statements

```
s = r ;
```

r = q ;
r -> link = s ;

Since **r** points to the first node, **s** would also point to the first node. Now **r** is assigned the value of **q** so that **r** now starts pointing to the second node. Finally **r -> link** is assigned with **s** so that **r -> link** starts pointing to the first node. But if we store the value of **s** in the **link** part of second node, then the address of the third node would be lost. Hence, before storing the value of **s** in **r -> link**, **q** is made to point to the third node through the statement

q = q -> link ;

While traversing the nodes through the **while** loop each time **q** starts pointing to the next node in the list and **r** starts pointing to the previous node. As a result, when the **while** loop ends all the links have been adjusted properly such that last node becomes the first node and first node becomes the last node.

Finally, once outside the **while** loop, the statement **p = r**, is executed. This ensures that the pointer **p** now starts pointing to the node, which is the last node of the original list. This is shown in Figure 3-8.

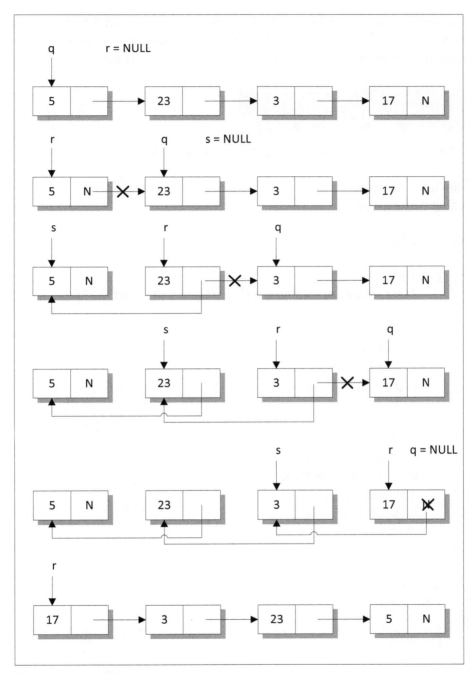

Figure 3-8. *Reversing the links.*

A Few More Operations

If you think carefully you can list out so many operations that can be performed on a linked list. For example, concatenating one linked list at the end of another, deleting all nodes present in a linked list, modifying certain elements in a linked list, etc. Given below is a program for concatenation of linked list and erasing all nodes in the list.

Honest Solid Code   {C++}

Program 3-3. Program to concatenate linked lists

```cpp
#include <iostream>
using namespace std ;

class linklist
{
    private :
        // structure containing a data part and a link part
        struct node
        {
            int data ;
            node *link ;
        } *p ;

    public :
        linklist( ) ;
        void append ( int num ) ;
        void concat ( linklist &l ) ;
        void display( ) ;
        int count( ) ;
        ~linklist( ) ;
} ;

// initializes data members
linklist :: linklist( )
{
    p = NULL ;
}

// adds a node at the end of a linked list
void linklist :: append ( int num )
{
    node *temp ;
```

```
        temp = p ;

        // if the list is empty, create first node
        if ( temp == NULL )
        {
            temp = new node ;
            p = temp ;
        }
        else
        {
            // go to last node
            while ( temp -> link != NULL )
                temp = temp -> link ;

            // add node at the end
            temp -> link = new node ;
            temp = temp -> link ;
        }
        // assign data to the last node
        temp -> data = num ;
        temp -> link = NULL ;
}

// concatenates two linked lists
void linklist :: concat ( linklist &l )
{
    node *temp ;

    // if the first linked list is empty
    if ( p == NULL )
        p = l.p ;

    else
    {
        // if both linked lists are non-empty
        if ( l.p != NULL )
        {
            // points to the starting of the first list
            temp = p ;

            // traverse the entire first linked list
```

```
            while ( temp -> link != NULL )
                temp = temp -> link ;

            // concatenate the second list after the first
            temp -> link = l.p ;
        }
    }
    l.p = NULL ;
}

// displays the contents of the linked list
void linklist :: display( )
{
    node *temp = p ;

    // traverse the entire linked list
    while ( temp != NULL )
    {
        cout << temp -> data << " " ;
        temp = temp -> link ;
    }
    cout << endl ;
}

// counts the number of nodes present in the linked list
int linklist :: count( )
{
    int c = 0 ;
    node *temp = p ;

    // traverse the entire linked list
    while ( temp != NULL )
    {
        temp = temp -> link ;
        c++ ;
    }
    return c ;
}

// deallocates memory
linklist :: ~linklist( )
```

```
{
    node *q ;
    while ( p != NULL )
    {
        q = p -> link ;
        delete p ;
        p = q ;
    }
}

int main( )
{
    linklist l1 ;
    l1.append ( 1 ) ; l1.append ( 2 ) ;
    l1.append ( 3 ) ; l1.append ( 4 ) ;
    cout << "Elements in 1st linked list: " << endl ;
    l1.display( ) ;
    cout << "No. of elements in 1st linked list: " << l1.count( ) << endl ;
    linklist l2 ;
    l2.append ( 5 ) ; l2.append ( 6 ) ;
    l2.append ( 7 ) ; l2.append ( 8 ) ;
    cout << "Elements in 2nd linked list: " << endl ;
    l2.display( ) ;
    cout << "No. of elements in 2nd linked list: " << l2.count( ) << endl ;
    // the result obtained after concatenation is in the first list
    l1.concat ( l2 ) ;
    cout << "Elements in 1st linked list after concatenation: " << endl ;
    l1.display( ) ;
    return 0 ;
}
```

Output:

Elements in 1st linked list:
1 2 3 4
No. of elements in 1st linked list: 4
Elements in 2nd linked list:
5 6 7 8
No. of elements in 2nd linked list: 4
Elements in 1st linked list after concatenation:
1 2 3 4 5 6 7 8

Recursive Operations on Linked List

In C++, it is possible for the functions to call themselves. A function is called 'recursive' if a statement within the body of a function calls the same function. Some of the operations that are carried out on linked lists can be easily implemented using recursion. These include counting the number of nodes present in a linked list, comparing two linked lists, copying one linked list into another, adding a new node at the end of the linked list, etc.

Given below is the program for carrying out each of these operations. The recursive functions in this program are pretty straight-forward. Hence, I would omit the discussion about working of each of them.

Honest Solid Code

Program 3-4. Recursive functions to count nodes in a linked list, comparing two linked lists, cloning a linked list and adding a new node at the end of a linked list

```cpp
#include <iostream>
using namespace std ;

class linklist
{
    private :
        // structure containing a data part and link part
        struct node
        {
            int data ;
            node *link ;
        } *p ;

    public :
        linklist( ) ;
        void add ( int num ) ;
        void addatend ( node **ptr, int num ) ;
        void display( ) ;
        int length( ) ;
        int getlength( node *ptr ) ;
        int operator == ( linklist &l ) ;
```

```
          int compare ( node *ptr1, node *ptr2 ) ;
          void copy ( linklist &l ) ;
          void duplicate ( node *ptr1, node **ptr2 ) ;
          ~linklist( ) ;
} ;

// initializes data memebr
linklist :: linklist( )
{
    p = NULL ;
}

void linklist :: add ( int num )
{
    addatend ( &p, num ) ;
}

// adds a new node at the end of the linked list
void linklist :: addatend ( node **ptr, int num )
{
    if ( *ptr == NULL )
    {
        (*ptr) = new node ;
        (*ptr) -> data = num ;
        (*ptr) -> link = NULL ;
    }
    else
        addatend ( &( ( *ptr ) -> link ), num ) ;
}

void linklist :: display( )
{
    node *temp = p ;
    // traverse the entire linked list
    while ( temp != NULL )
    {
        cout << temp -> data  << " " ;
        temp = temp -> link ;
    }
    cout << endl ;
}
```

```
int linklist :: length( )
{
    return getlength( p ) ;
}

// counts the number of nodes in a linked list
int linklist :: getlength ( node *ptr )
{
    int l ;

    // if list is empty or if NULL is encountered
    if ( ptr == NULL )
        return ( 0 ) ;
    else
    {
        // go to next node
        l = 1 + getlength ( ptr -> link ) ;
        return ( l ) ;
    }
}

// calls compare
int linklist :: operator == ( linklist &l )
{
    return compare ( p, l.p ) ;
}

// compares 2 linked lists and returns 1 if
// linked lists are equal and 0 if unequal
int linklist :: compare ( node *q, node *r )
{
    if ( q == NULL  &&  r == NULL  )
        return 1 ;
    else
    {
        if ( q == NULL || r == NULL )
            return 0 ;
        else if ( q -> data != r -> data )
            return 0 ;
        else
```

```
            compare ( q -> link, r -> link ) ;
    }
}

// calls copy to copy a linked list into another
void linklist :: copy ( linklist &l )
{
    duplicate ( l.p, &p ) ;
}

// copies a linked list into another
void linklist :: duplicate ( node *ptr1, node **ptr2 )
{
    if ( ptr1 != NULL )
    {
        *ptr2 = new node ;
        (*ptr2) -> data = ptr1 -> data ;
        (*ptr2) -> link = NULL ;
        duplicate ( ptr1 -> link, &( ( *ptr2 ) -> link ) ) ;
    }
}

// deallocates memory
linklist :: ~linklist( )
{
    node *q ;
    while ( p != NULL )
    {
        q = p -> link ;
        delete p ;
        p = q ;
    }
}

int main( )
{
    linklist l1 ;
    l1.add ( 1 ) ;
    l1.add ( 2 ) ;
    l1.add ( 3 ) ;
    l1.add ( 4 ) ;
```

```
        l1.display( ) ;
        cout << "Length of linked list: " << l1.length( ) << endl ;

        linklist l2 ;
        l2.add ( 1 ) ;
        l2.add ( 2 ) ;
        l2.add ( 3 ) ;
        l2.display( ) ;

        if ( l1 == l2 )
            cout << "Both linked lists are equal" << endl ;
        else
            cout << "Both linked lists are different" << endl ;

        linklist l3 ;
        l3.copy ( l1 ) ;
        l3.display( ) ;
        return 0 ;
}
```

Output:

```
1 2 3 4
Length of linked list: 4
1 2 3
Both linked lists are different
1 2 3 4
```

Doubly Linked Lists

In the linked lists that we have used so far each node provides information about where is the next node in the list. It has no knowledge about where the previous node lies in memory. If we are at say the 15th node in the list, then to reach the 14th node we have to traverse the list right from the first node. To avoid this we can store in each node not only the address of next node but also the address of the previous node in the linked list. This arrangement is often known as a 'Doubly Linked List' and is shown in Figure 3-9.

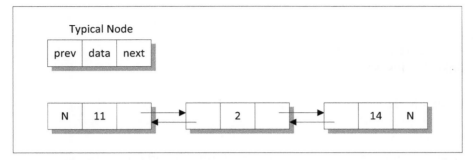

Figure 3-9. *Doubly linked list.*

The following program implements the Doubly Linked List (DLL).

Honest Solid Code

{C++}

Program 3-4. Program to implement a doubly linked list

```cpp
#include <iostream>
using namespace std ;

class linklist
{
    private :
        // structure representing a node of the doubly linked list
        struct dnode
        {
            dnode *prev ;
            int data ;
            dnode * next ;
        } *p ;

    public :
        linklist( ) ;
        void d_append ( int num ) ;
        void d_addatbeg ( int num ) ;
        void d_addafter ( int loc, int num ) ;
        void d_display( ) ;
        int d_count( ) ;
        void d_delete( int i ) ;
        ~linklist( ) ;
```

```cpp
} ;

// initializes data member
linklist :: linklist( )
{
    p = NULL ;
}

// adds a new node at the end of the doubly linked list
void linklist :: d_append ( int num )
{
    dnode *r, *q ;
    q = p ;

    // if the linked list is empty
    if ( q == NULL )
    {
        //create a new node
        q = new dnode ;
        q -> prev = NULL ;
        q -> data = num ;
        q -> next = NULL ;
        p = q ;
    }
    else
    {
        // traverse the linked list till the last node is reached
        while ( q -> next != NULL )
            q = q -> next ;

        // add a new node at the end
        r = new dnode ;
        r -> data = num ;
        r -> next = NULL ;
        r -> prev = q ;
        q -> next = r ;
    }
}

// adds a new node at the begining of the linked list
void linklist :: d_addatbeg ( int num )
```

```
{
    dnode *q ;

    // create a new node
    q = new dnode ;
    q -> prev = NULL ;
    q -> data = num ;
    q -> next = p ;

    // make new node the head node
    p -> prev = q ;
    p = q ;
}

// adds a new node after the specified number of nodes
void linklist :: d_addafter ( int loc, int num )
{
    dnode *q ;
    q = p ;

    // skip to desired portion
    for ( int i = 0 ; i < loc ; i++ )
    {
        q = q -> next ;
        // if end of linked list is encountered
        if ( q == NULL )
        {
            cout << "There are less than " << loc << " elements" << endl ;
            return ;
        }
    }

    // insert new node
    q = q -> prev ;
    dnode *temp = new dnode ;
    temp -> data = num ;
    temp -> prev = q ;
    temp -> next = q -> next ;
    temp -> next -> prev = temp ;
    q -> next = temp ;
}
```

```
// displays the contents of the linked list
void linklist :: d_display( )
{
    dnode *temp = p ;
    // traverse the entire linked list
    while ( temp != NULL )
    {
        cout << temp -> data << " " ;
        temp = temp -> next ;
    }
    cout << endl ;
}

// counts the number of nodes present in the linked list
int linklist :: d_count( )
{
    int c = 0 ;
    dnode *temp = p ;

    // traverse the entire linked list
    while ( temp != NULL )
    {
        temp = temp -> next ;
        c++ ;
    }
    return c ;
}

// deletes the specified node from the doubly linked list
void linklist :: d_delete ( int num )
{
    dnode *q = p ;

    // traverse the entire linked list
    while ( q != NULL )
    {
        // if node to be deleted is found
        if ( q -> data == num )
        {
            // if node to be deleted is the first node
```

```
            if ( q == p )
            {
                p = p -> next ;
                p -> prev = NULL ;
            }
            else
            {
                // if node to be deleted is the last node
                if ( q -> next == NULL )
                    q -> prev -> next = NULL ;
                else
                // if node to be deleted is any intermediate node
                {
                    q -> prev -> next = q -> next ;
                    q -> next -> prev = q -> prev ;
                }
                delete q ;
            }

            // return back after deletion
            return ;
        }

        // go to next node
        q = q -> next ;
    }
    cout << num << " not found" << endl ;
}

// deallocates memory
linklist :: ~linklist( )
{
    dnode *q ;
    while ( p -> next != NULL )
    {
        q = p -> next ;
        delete p ;
        p = q ;
    }
}
```

```
int main( )
{
    linklist l ;
    l.d_append ( 11 ) ; l.d_append ( 2 ) ;
    l.d_append ( 14 ) ; l.d_append ( 17 ) ;
    l.d_append ( 99 ) ;

    cout << "Elements in DLL: " << endl ;
    l.d_display( ) ;
    cout << "No. of elements: " << l.d_count( ) << endl ;

    l.d_addatbeg ( 33 ) ; l.d_addatbeg ( 55 ) ;
    cout << "Elements in DLL after addition at the beginning: " ;
    l.d_display( ) ;
    cout << "No. of elements: " << l.d_count( ) << endl ;

    l.d_addafter ( 4, 66 ) ;  l.d_addafter ( 2, 96 ) ;
    cout << "Elements in DLL after addition at given position: " << endl ;
    l.d_display( ) ;
    cout << "No. of elements: " << l.d_count( ) << endl ;

    l.d_delete ( 55 ) ; l.d_delete ( 2 ) ; l.d_delete ( 99 ) ;
    cout << "Elements in DLL after deletion: " << endl ;
    l.d_display( ) ;
    cout << "No. of elements: " << l.d_count( ) << endl ;
    return 0 ;
}
```

Let us now understand the different functions that we have defined in the program. Let us begin with the one that appends a new node at the end of a double linked list.

Function *d_append( )*

The **d_append( )** function adds a node at the end of the existing list. It also checks the special case of adding the first node if the list is empty. This function accepts a parameter **num**, which holds an integer to be added to the list.

To begin with we initialize **q** which is of the type **struct dnode *** with the value stored at **p**. This is done because using **q** the entire list is traversed if it is non-empty.

If the list is empty then the condition

if (q == NULL)

gets satisfied. Now memory is allocated for the new node whose address is stored in **q** (i.e. **p**). Using **q** a **NULL** value is stored in its **prev** and **next** links and the value of **num** is assigned to its **data** part.

If the list is non-empty then through the statements

while (q -> next != NULL)
    q = q -> next ;

q is made to point to the last node of the list. Then memory is allocated for the node whose address is stored in **r**. A **NULL** value is stored in the **next** part of this node, because this is going to be last node. Now what remains to be done is to link this node with rest of the list. This is done through the statements

r -> prev = q ;
q -> next = r ;

The statement **r -> prev = q** makes the **prev** part of the new node **r** to point to the previous node **q**. The statement **q -> next = r** makes the **next** part of **q** to point to the last node **r**. This is shown in Figure 3-10.

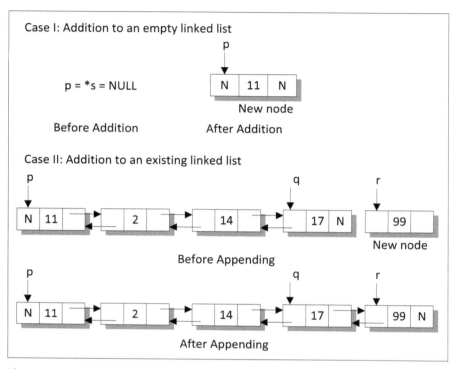

Figure 3-10. *Addition of a node to a Doubly linked list.*

Function *d_addatbeg( )*

The **d_addatbeg( )** function adds a node at the beginning of the existing list. This function too accepts parameter **num**, which holds an integer to be added to the list.

Memory is allocated for the new node whose address is stored in **q**. Then **num** is stored in the **data** part of the new node. A **NULL** value is stored in **prev** part of the new node as this is going to be the first node of the list. The **next** part of this new node should contain the address of the first node of the list. This is done through the statement

q -> next = p ;

Now what remains to be done is to store the address of this new node into the **prev** part of the first node and make this new node the first node in the list. This is done through the statements

p -> prev = q ;
p = q ;

These operations are shown in Figure 3-11.

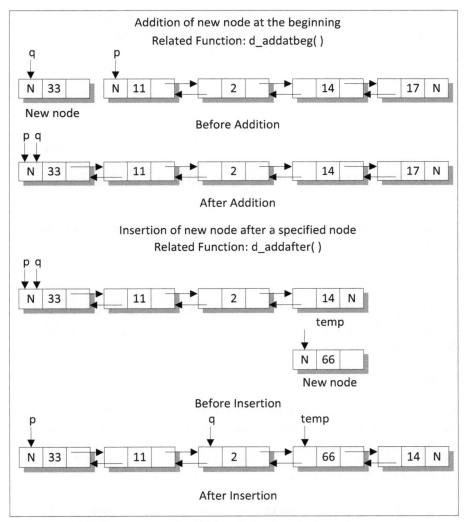

Figure 3-11. *Working of d_addatbeg( ) and d_addafter( ).*

Function *d_addafter( )*

The **d_addafter( )** function adds a node at the specified position of an existing list. This operation of adding a new node in between two existing nodes can be better understood with the help of Figure 3-11.

This function accepts two parameters. The first parameter **loc** specifies the node number after which the new node must be inserted. The second parameter **num** is an integer, which is to be added to the list.

A loop is executed to reach the position where the node is to be added. This loop also checks whether the position **loc** that we have mentioned, really occurs in the list or not. When the loop ends, we reach the **loc** position where the node is to be inserted. By this time **q** is pointing to the node before which the new node is to be added.

The statement

q = q -> prev ;

makes **q** to point to the node after which the new node should be added. Then memory is allocated for the new node and its address is stored in **temp**. The value of **num** is stored in the **data** part of the new node.

The **prev** part of the new node should point to **q**. This is done through the statement

temp -> prev = q ;

The **next** part of the new node should point to the node whose address is stored in the **next** part of node pointed to by **q**. This is achieved through the statement

temp -> next = q -> next ;

Now what remains to be done is to make **prev** part of the next node (node pointed by **q -> next**) to point to the new node. This is done through the statement

temp -> next -> prev = temp ;

At the end, we change the **next** part of the **q** to make it point to the new node, and this is done through the statement

q -> next = temp ;

Function *d_delete( )*

The function **d_delete( )** deletes a node from the list if the **data** part of that node matches **num**. This function receives the number that is to be deleted from the list.

We run a loop to traverse the list. Inside the loop the **data** part of each node is compared with the **num** value. If the **num** value matches the **data** part in the node then we need to check the position of the node to be deleted.

If it happens to be the first node, then the first node is made to point to the **next** part of the first node. This is done through the statement

p = p -> next ;

Then, a value **NULL** is stored in **prev** part of the second node, since it is now going to become the first node. This is done through the statement

p -> prev = NULL ;

If the node to be deleted happens to be the last node, then **NULL** is stored in the **next** part of the second last node. This is done through the statements

if (q -> next == NULL)
    q -> prev -> next = NULL ;

If the node to be deleted happens to be any intermediate node, then the address of the next node is stored in the **next** part of the previous node and the address of the previous node is stored in the **prev** part of the next node. This is done through the statements

q -> prev -> next = q -> next ;
q -> next -> prev = q -> prev ;

Finally the memory occupied by the node being deleted is released by using the **delete** operator. Figure 3-12 shows the working of the **d_delete( )** function.

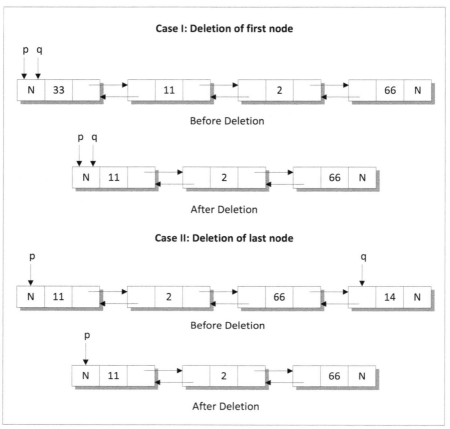

Figure 3-12. *Working of **d_delete( )** function.*

Chapter Bullets

Summary of chapter

(a) Linked List is a linear data structure used to store similar data.

(b) Unlike an array, in a linked list there's no need to specify how many elements you're going to store ahead of time. One can keep adding elements as long as there's enough memory in the machine.

(c) Linked list is implemented using structure data type.

(d) Linked list may be singly linked or doubly linked.

(e) Singly linked lists have a single pointer pointing to the next node in the list. The last pointer is empty or points to null, signaling the end of the list.

(f)   Doubly linked lists have two pointers, one pointing to the next node and one pointing to the previous node. The first node's previous pointer points to null and the last node's next pointer points to null to signal the end of the list.

Check Your Progress

Exercise - Level I

[A] State whether the following statements are True or False:

(a)   Linked list is used to store similar data.

(b)   All nodes in the linked may be in non-contiguous memory locations.

(c)   The link part of the last node in a singly linked list always contains **NULL**.

(d)   In a singly linked list, if we lose the location of the first node it is as good as having lost the entire linked list.

(e)   Doubly linked list facilitates movement from one node to another in either direction.

(f)   A doubly linked list will occupy less memory as compared to a corresponding singly linked list.

(g)   If we are to traverse from first node to last node it would be faster to do so if the linked list is singly linked instead of doubly linked.

(h)   In a structure used to represent the node of a doubly linked list it is necessary that the structure elements are in the order backward link, data, forward link.

Sharpen Your Skills

Exercise - Level II

[B] Answer the Following:

(a)   Write a program that reads the name, age and salary of 10 persons and maintains them in a linked list sorted by name.

(b)   There are two linked lists **A** and **B** containing the following data:
       A: 3, 7, 10, 15, 16, 9, 22, 17, 32

B: 16, 2, 9, 13, 37, 8, 10, 1, 28

Write a program to create:

- A linked list **C** that contains only those elements that are common in linked list **A** and **B**.

- A linked list **D** which contains all elements of **A** as well as **B** ensuring that there is no repetition of elements.

(c) There are two linked lists **A** and **B** containing the following data:

A: 7, 5, 3, 1, 20
B: 6, 25, 32, 11, 9

Write a function to combine the two lists such that the resulting list contains nodes in the following elements:

7, 6, 5, 25, 3, 32, 1, 11, 20, 9

You are not allowed to create any additional node while writing the function.

Coding Interview Questions

Exercise Level III

(a) A linked list contains some positive numbers and some negative numbers. Using this linked list write a program to create two new linked lists, one containing all positive numbers and the other containing all negative numbers.

(b) Write a program to delete duplicate elements in a linked list.

Case Scenario Exercise

Polynomials using Linked List

Polynomials like $5x^4 + 2x^3 + 7x^2 + 10x - 8$ can be maintained using a linked list. To achieve this each node should consist of three elements, namely coefficient, exponent and a link to the next term. Assume that the exponent of each successive term is less than that of the previous term. Write a program to build a linked list to represent a polynomial and perform common polynomial operations like addition and multiplication.

04
Chapter

Sparse Matrices
Lean Is Better

Why This Chapter Matters?

Computer's memory is a costly resource. We have
to use it judiciously. Sparse matrices often eat away
lot of costly memory space. This chapter explains
how to conserve this memory and still work with
matrices as usual.

7 1 percent of earth is occupied by water, leaving a meagerly 29 percent for land. It is only natural that we need to conserve the available space. Nobody should occupy more space than what they deserve to occupy, be it animals, man, plants or matrices. There is no point in wasting costly space in computer's memory in storing elements that do not deserve a place in it. Sparse matrix is the case in point.

If many elements from a matrix have a value 0 then the matrix is known as a **sparse matrix**. There is no precise definition of when a matrix is sparse and when it is not, but it is a concept, which we can all recognize intuitively. If the matrix is sparse we must consider an alternate way of representing it rather than the normal row major or column major arrangement. This is because if majority of elements of the matrix are 0 then an alternative through which we can store only the non-zero elements and keep intact the functionality of the matrix can save a lot of memory space. Figure 4-1 shows a sparse matrix of dimension 7x7.

		Columns						
		0	1	2	3	4	5	6
	0	0	0	0	5	0	0	0
	1	0	4	0	0	0	0	7
	2	0	0	0	0	9	0	0
Rows	3	0	3	0	2	0	0	0
	4	1	0	2	0	0	0	0
	5	0	0	0	0	0	0	0
	6	0	0	8	0	0	0	0

Figure 4-1. *Representation of a sparse matrix of dimension 7 x 7.*

A common way of representing non-zero elements of a sparse matrix is the 3-tuple forms. In this form each non-zero element is stored in a row, with the 1st and 2nd element of this row containing the row and column in which the element is present in the original matrix. The 3rd element in this row stores the actual value of the non-zero element. For example the 3-tuple representation of the sparse matrix shown in Figure 4-1 is shown below.

```
int spmat[ 10 ][ 3 ] = {
                            7, 7, 9,
                            0, 3, -5,
                            1, 1, 4,
                            1, 6, 7,
                            2, 4, 9,
                            3, 1, 3,
                            3, 3, 2,
                            4, 0, 11,
                            4, 2, 2,
                            6, 2, 8
                        }
```

There are two ways in which information of a 3-tuple can be stored:

— Arrays
— Linked List

In both representations information about the non-zero elements is stored. However, as the number of non-zero elements in a sparse matrix may vary, it would be efficient to use a linked list to represent it.

Representation of Sparse Matrix as an Array

Let us see a program that accepts elements of a sparse matrix and creates an array containing 3-tuples of non-zero elements present in the sparse matrix.

Honest Solid Code   {C++}

Program 4-1. Sparse Matrix in 3-tuple form

```cpp
#include <iostream>
using namespace std ;
const int MAX1 = 3 ;
const int MAX2 = 3 ;

class sparse
{
    private :
        int *sp ;
        int row ;
```

```
    public :
        sparse( ) ;
        void create_array( ) ;
        void display( ) ;
         int count( ) ;
        void create_tuple ( sparse &s ) ;
        void display_tuple( ) ;
        ~sparse( ) ;
} ;

// initialises data members
sparse :: sparse( )
{
    sp = NULL ;
}

// dynamically creates the matrix of size MAX1 x MAX2
void sparse :: create_array( )
{
    int n ;
    sp = new int [ MAX1 * MAX2 ] ;
    for ( int i = 0 ; i < MAX1 * MAX2 ; i++ )
    {
            cout << "Enter element no. " << i << ": " ;
            cin >> n ;
            * ( sp + i ) = n ;
    }
}

// displays the contents of the matrix
void sparse :: display( )
{
    // traverses the entire matrix
    for ( int i = 0 ; i < MAX1 * MAX2 ; i++ )
    {
        // positions the cursor to the new line for every new row
        if ( i % MAX2 == 0 )
            cout << endl ;
        cout << * ( sp + i ) << " " ;
    }
}
```

```
// counts the number of non-zero elements
int sparse :: count( )
{
    int cnt = 0 ;
    for ( int i = 0 ; i < MAX1 * MAX2 ; i++ )
    {
        if ( * ( sp + i ) != 0 )
            cnt++ ;
    }
    return cnt ;
}

// creates an array that stores information about non-zero elements
void sparse :: create_tuple ( sparse &s )
{
    int r = 0 , c = -1, l = -1 ;

    row = s.count( ) + 1 ;
    sp = new int[ row * 3 ] ;
    * ( sp + 0 ) = MAX1 ;
    * ( sp + 1 ) = MAX2 ;
    * ( sp + 2 ) = row - 1 ;

    l = 2 ;
    for ( int i = 0 ; i < MAX1 * MAX2 ; i++ )
    {
        c++ ;
        // sets the row and column values
        if ( ( ( i % MAX2 ) == 0 ) && ( i != 0 ) )
        {
            r++ ;
            c = 0 ;
        }
        // check for non-zero element
        // assign row, column and non-zero element value
        if ( * ( s.sp + i ) != 0 )
        {
            l++ ;
            * ( sp + l ) = r ;
            l++ ;
```

```
            * ( sp + I ) = c ;
            I++ ;
            * ( sp + I ) = * ( s.sp + i ) ;
        }
    }
}

// displays the contents of 3-tuple
void sparse :: display_tuple( )
{
    for ( int i = 0 ; i < row * 3 ; i++ )
    {
        if ( i % 3 == 0 )
            cout << endl ;
        cout << * ( sp + i ) << " " ;
    }
}

// deallocates memory
sparse :: ~sparse( )
{
    delete sp ;
}

int main( )
{
    sparse s1 ;
    s1.create_array( ) ;
    cout << endl << "Elements in Sparse Matrix: " ;
    s1.display( ) ;
    int c = s1.count( ) ;
    cout << "\n\nNumber of non-zero elements: " << c ;
    sparse s2 ;
    s2.create_tuple ( s1 ) ;
    cout << "\n\nArray of non-zero elements: " ;
    s2.display_tuple( ) ;
    return 0 ;
}
```

Output:
Enter element no. 0: 0

Enter element no. 1: 2
Enter element no. 2: 0
Enter element no. 3: 9
Enter element no. 4: 0
Enter element no. 5: 1
Enter element no. 6: 0
Enter element no. 7: 0
Enter element no. 8: -4

Elements in Sparse Matrix:
0 2 0
9 0 1
0 0 -4

Number of non-zero elements: 4

Array of non-zero elements:
3 3 4
0 1 2
1 0 9
1 2 1
2 2 -4

In this program we have designed a class called **sparse**. In the **create_array( )** function, we have dynamically created a matrix of size **MAX1** x **MAX2**. The values for the matrix are accepted through keyboard. The **display( )** function displays the contents of the sparse matrix and the **count( )** function counts the total number of non-zero elements present in sparse matrix.

The **create_tuple( )** function creates a 2-D array dynamically. But, the question arises as how much space should get allocated for this array? Since each row in the 3-tuple form represents a non-zero element in the original array the new array should contain as many rows as the number of non-zero elements in the original matrix. From the 3-tuple form we must be able to build the original array. Hence the very first row in the new array should contain number of row, number of columns and number of non-zero elements in the original array. In the program we have determined the size of the new array through the following statements:

row = s.count( ) + 1 ;

```
sp = new int[ row * 3 ] ;
```

In the first statement we have obtained the count of non-zero elements present in the given array. To that count we have added 1. The first row (i.e. 0th row) in this array stores the information about the total number of rows, columns and non-zero elements present in the given array. From second row (i.e. 1st row) onwards this array stores the row and column position of a non-zero element and the value of the non-zero element. Since the number of rows in the array depends on the number of non-zero elements in the given array we have created the array dynamically. The number of columns in this array would always be 3. The 0th column stores the row number of the non-zero element. The 1st column stores the column number of the non-zero element and the 2nd column stores the value of non-zero element.

Lastly, the **display_tuple( )** function displays the contents of 3-tuple.

Common Matrix Operations

Common matrix operations are addition, multiplication, transposition, etc. Let us see how these operations are carried out on a sparse matrix implemented as an array. Note that each program that we are going to discuss now consists of functions—**create_array( )**, **create_tuple( )**, **display( )**, **display_tuple( )** and **count( )**. We have already seen the working of these functions in previous program. Hence we shall discuss only the function(s) that perform given matrix operation.

Transpose of a Sparse Matrix

Following program accepts elements of a sparse matrix, creates a 3-tuple form of non-zero elements present in the sparse matrix and then obtains a transpose of the sparse matrix from the 3-tuple form.

Honest Solid Code   {C++}

Program 4-2. Transpose of a Sparse Matrix

```
#include <iostream>
using namespace std ;
const int MAX1 = 3 ;
const int MAX2 = 3 ;

class sparse
```

```
{
    private :
        int *sp ;
        int row ;
    public :
        sparse( ) ;
        void create_array( ) ;
        void display( ) ;
        int count( ) ;
        void create_tuple ( sparse &s ) ;
        void display_tuple( ) ;
        void transpose ( sparse &s ) ;
        void display_transpose( ) ;
        ~sparse( ) ;
} ;

// initialises data members
sparse :: sparse( )
{
    sp = NULL ;
}

// creates the matrix of size MAX1 x MAX2
void sparse :: create_array( )
{
    int n ;
    sp = new int [ MAX1 * MAX2 ] ;
    for ( int i = 0 ; i < MAX1 * MAX2 ; i++ )
    {
        cout << "Enter element no. " << i << ": " ;
        cin >> n ;
        * ( sp + i ) = n ;
    }
}

// displays the contents of the matrix
void sparse :: display( )
{
    // traverses the entire matrix
    for ( int i = 0 ; i < MAX1 * MAX2 ; i++ )
    {
```

```
        // positions the cursor to the new line for every new row
        if ( i % MAX2 == 0 )
            cout << endl ;
        cout << * ( sp + i ) << " " ;
    }
}

// counts the number of non-zero elements
int sparse :: count( )
{
    int cnt = 0 ;
    for ( int i = 0 ; i < MAX1 * MAX2 ; i++ )
    {
        if ( * ( sp + i ) != 0 )
            cnt++ ;
    }
    return cnt ;
}

// creates an array that stores information about non-zero elements
void sparse :: create_tuple ( sparse &s )
{
    int r = 0 , c = -1, l = -1 ;

    row = s.count( ) + 1 ;
    sp = new int[ row * 3 ] ;
    * ( sp + 0 ) = MAX1 ;
    * ( sp + 1 ) = MAX2 ;
    * ( sp + 2 ) = row - 1 ;

    l = 2 ;
    for ( int i = 0 ; i < MAX1 * MAX2 ; i++ )
    {
        c++ ;
        // sets the row and column values
        if ( ( ( i % MAX2 ) == 0 ) && ( i != 0 ) )
        {
            r++ ;
            c = 0 ;
        }
```

```
            // check for non-zero element
            // assign row, column and non-zero element value
            if ( * ( s.sp + i ) != 0 )
            {
                l++ ;
                * ( sp + l ) = r ;
                l++ ;
                * ( sp + l ) = c ;
                l++ ;
                * ( sp + l ) = * ( s.sp + i ) ;
            }
        }
}

// obtains transpose of an array
void sparse :: transpose ( sparse &s )
{
    sp = new int[ s.row * 3 ] ;
    row = s.row ;

    * ( sp + 0 ) = * ( s.sp + 1 ) ;
    * ( sp + 1 ) = * ( s.sp + 0 ) ;
    * ( sp + 2 ) = * ( s.sp + 2 ) ;

    int col = * ( sp + 1 ) ;
    int elem = * ( sp + 2 ) ;

    if ( elem <= 0 )
        return ;

    int x, y, c, p, pos_1, pos_2 ;
    x = 1 ;
    for ( c = 0 ; c < col ; c++ )
    {
        for ( y = 1 ; y <= elem ; y++ )
        {
            p = y * 3 + 1 ;
            if ( * ( s.sp + p ) == c )
            {
                pos_2 = x * 3 + 0 ;
                pos_1 = y * 3 + 1 ;
```

```
                * ( sp + pos_2 ) = * ( s.sp + pos_1 ) ;
                pos_2 = x * 3 + 1 ;
                pos_1 = y * 3 + 0 ;
                * ( sp + pos_2 ) = * ( s.sp + pos_1 ) ;
                pos_2 = x * 3 + 2 ;
                pos_1 = y * 3 + 2 ;
                * ( sp + pos_2 ) = * ( s.sp + pos_1 ) ;
                x++ ;
            }
        }
    }
}

// displays the contents of 3-tuple
void sparse :: display_tuple( )
{
    for ( int i = 0 ; i < row * 3 ; i++ )
    {
        if ( i % 3 == 0 )
            cout << endl ;
        cout << * ( sp + i ) << " " ;
    }
}

// displays 3-tuple after transpose operation
void sparse :: display_transpose( )
{
    for ( int i = 0 ; i < row * 3 ; i++ )
    {
        if ( i % 3 == 0 )
            cout << endl ;
        cout << * ( sp + i ) << " " ;
    }
}

// deallocates memory
sparse :: ~sparse( )
{
    delete sp ;
}
```

```
int main( )
{
    sparse s1 ;
    s1.create_array( ) ;
    cout << endl << "Elements in Sparse Matrix: " ;
    s1.display( ) ;
    int c = s1.count( ) ;
    cout << "\n\nNumber of non-zero elements: " << c ;
    sparse s2 ;
    s2.create_tuple ( s1 ) ;
    cout << "\n\nArray of non-zero elements: " ;
    s2.display_tuple( ) ;
    sparse s3 ;
    s3.transpose ( s2 ) ;
    cout << "\n\nTranspose of array: " ;
    s3.display_transpose( ) ;
    return 0 ;
}
```

Output:
Enter element no. 0: 4
Enter element no. 1: 0
Enter element no. 2: 1
Enter element no. 3: 0
Enter element no. 4: 0
Enter element no. 5: 3
Enter element no. 6: -2
Enter element no. 7: 0
Enter element no. 8: 0

Elements in Sparse Matrix:
4 0 1
0 0 3
-2 0 0

Number of non-zero elements: 4

Array of non-zero elements:
3 3 4
0 0 4
0 2 1

1 2 3
2 0 -2

Transpose of array:
3 3 4
0 0 4
0 2 -2
2 0 1
2 1 3

In the **transpose( )** function first we have allocated memory required to store the elements in the target 3-tuple. Next we have stored the total number of rows, columns and non-zero elements that this 3-tuple will hold. This is achieved through the following three statements:

```
* ( sp + 0 ) = * ( s.sp + 1 ) ;
* ( sp + 1 ) = * ( s.sp + 0 ) ;
* ( sp + 2 ) = * ( s.sp + 2 ) ;
```

Note that, here in **sp**, the place where total number of rows should get stored we have stored total number of columns. Similarly in place where total number of columns should get stored we have stored total number of rows. This is because in case of transpose operation total number rows become equal to total number of columns and vice versa.

The transpose operation is carried out through a pair of **for** loops. The outer **for** loop runs till the non-zero elements of **col** number of columns (of source 3-tuple) are not scanned. In the inner **for** loop first we have obtained the position at which the column number of a non-zero element is stored (in the source 3-tuple) through the statement:

p = y * 3 + 1 ;

Then we have checked whether the column number of a non-zero element matches with the column number currently being considered i.e. **c**. If the two values match then the information is stored in the target 3-tuple through the statements given below:

```
pos_2 = x * 3 + 0 ;
pos_1 = y * 3 + 1 ;
* ( sp + pos_2 ) = * ( s.sp + pos_1 ) ;
```

The variable **pos_2** is used for the target 3-tuple, to store the position at which data from source 3-tuple should get copied. Similarly, the variable

pos_1 is used for the source 3-tuple, to extract data from it. The third statement copies the column position of a non-zero element from source 3-tuple to the target 3-tuple. This column number gets stored at the row position in target 3-tuple.

On similar lines the row position of a non-zero element of source 3-tuple is copied at the column position of the target 3-tuple through the following statements:

```
pos_2 = x * 3 + 1 ;
pos_1 = y * 3 + 0 ;
* ( sp + pos_2 ) = * ( s.sp + pos_1 ) ;
```

Finally, the non-zero value from source 3-tuple is copied to the target 3-tuple through the following statements:

```
pos_2 = x * 3 + 2 ;
pos_1 = y * 3 + 2 ;
* ( sp + pos_2 ) = * ( s.sp + pos_1 ) ;
```

The target 3-tuple thus obtained is nothing but a transpose of an array that user has entered through **create_array( )** function. But the target 3-tuple stores the information of non-zero elements. The elements in this 3-tuple are then displayed by calling **display_transpose( )** function.

Addition of Sparse Matrices

Let us now see a program that carries out addition of two sparse matrices represented in 3-tuple form. Here is the program...

Honest Solid Code   {C++}

Program 4-3. Addition of Sparse Matrices

```cpp
#include <iostream>
using namespace std ;
const int MAX1 = 3 ;
const int MAX2 = 3 ;
const int MAXSIZE = 9 ;
const int BIGNUM = 100 ;

class sparse
```

```
{
    private :
        int *sp ;
        int row ;
        int *result ;
    public :
        sparse( ) ;
        void create_array( ) ;
        int count( ) ;
        void display( ) ;
        void create_tuple ( sparse &s ) ;
        void display_tuple( ) ;
        void addmat ( sparse &s1, sparse &s2 ) ;
        void display_result( ) ;
        ~sparse( ) ;
} ;

// initialises data members
sparse :: sparse( )
{
    sp = NULL ;
    result = NULL ;
}

// dynamically creates the matrix
void sparse :: create_array( )
{
    int n ;
    // allocate memory
    sp = new int [ MAX1 * MAX2 ] ;
    // add elements to the array
    cout << endl ;
    for ( int i = 0 ; i < MAX1 * MAX2 ; i++ )
    {
            cout << "Enter element no. " << i << ": " ;
            cin >> n ;
            * ( sp + i ) = n ;
    }
}
```

// displays the contents of the matrix

```
void sparse :: display( )
{
    // traverses the entire matrix
    for ( int i = 0 ; i < MAX1 * MAX2 ; i++ )
    {
        // positions the cursor to the new line for every new row
        if ( i % MAX2 == 0 )
            cout << endl ;
        cout << * ( sp + i ) << " " ;
    }
}

// counts the number of non-zero elements
int sparse :: count( )
{
    int cnt = 0 ;
    for ( int i = 0 ; i < MAX1 * MAX2 ; i++ )
    {
        if ( * ( sp + i ) != 0 )
            cnt++ ;
    }
    return cnt ;
}

// creates an array that stores information about non-zero elements
void sparse :: create_tuple ( sparse &s )
{
    int r = 0 , c = -1, l = -1 ;

    // get the total number of non-zero elements
    // add 1 to store total no. of rows, cols, and non-zero values
    row = s.count( ) + 1 ;

    // allocate memory
    sp = new int[ row * 3 ] ;

    // store information about
    // total no. of rows, cols, and non-zero values
    * ( sp + 0 ) = MAX1 ;
    * ( sp + 1 ) = MAX2 ;
    * ( sp + 2 ) = row - 1 ;
```

```
l = 2 ;
// scan the array and store info. about non-zero values
// in the 3-tuple
for ( int i = 0 ; i < MAX1 * MAX2 ; i++ )
{
    c++ ;

    // sets the row and column values
    if ( ( ( i % MAX2 ) == 0 ) && ( i != 0 ) )
    {
        r++ ;
        c = 0 ;
    }

    // checks for non-zero element
    // stores row, column and non-zero element value
    if ( * ( s.sp + i ) != 0 )
    {
        l++ ;
        * ( sp + l ) = r ;
        l++ ;
        * ( sp + l ) = c ;
        l++ ;
        * ( sp + l ) = * ( s.sp + i ) ;
    }
}
}

// displays the contents of the matrix
void sparse :: display_tuple( )
{
    // traverses the entire matrix
    cout << "\nElements in a 3-tuple: " << endl ;
    int j = ( * ( sp + 2 ) * 3 ) + 3 ;
    for ( int i = 0 ; i < j ; i++ )
    {
        // positions the cursor to the new line for every new row
        if ( i % 3 == 0 )
            cout << endl ;
        cout << * ( sp + i ) << " " ;
```

```
        }
        cout << endl ;
}

// carries out addition of two matrices
void sparse :: addmat ( sparse &s1, sparse &s2 )
{
    int i = 1, j = 1, k = 1 ;
    int elem = 1 ;
    int max, amax, bmax ;
    int rowa, rowb, cola, colb, vala, valb ;

    // get the total number of non-zero values
    // from both the matrices
    amax = * ( s1.sp + 2 ) ;
    bmax = * ( s2.sp + 2 ) ;
    max = amax + bmax ;

    // allocate memory for result
    result = new int[ MAXSIZE*3 ] ;

    while ( elem <= max )
    {
        // check if i <= max.
        // get info. about non-zero values in first 3-tuple
        if ( i <= amax )
        {
            rowa = * ( s1.sp + i * 3 + 0 ) ;
            cola = * ( s1.sp + i * 3 + 1 ) ;
            vala = * ( s1.sp + i * 3 + 2 ) ;
        }
        else
            rowa = cola = BIGNUM ;

        // check if j <= max. non-zero values
        // get info. about non-zero values in second 3-tuple
        if ( j <= bmax )
        {
            rowb = * ( s2.sp + j * 3 + 0 ) ;
            colb = * ( s2.sp + j * 3 + 1 ) ;
            valb = * ( s2.sp + j * 3 + 2 ) ;
```

```
        }
        else
            rowb = colb = BIGNUM ;

        // if row no. of both 3-tuple are same
        if ( rowa == rowb )
        {
            // if col no. of both 3-tuple are same
            if ( cola == colb )
            {
                // add tow non-zero values
                // store in result
                * ( result + k * 3 + 0 ) = rowa ;
                * ( result + k * 3 + 1 ) = cola ;
                * ( result + k * 3 + 2 ) = vala + valb ;
                i++ ;
                j++ ;
                max-- ;
            }

            // if col no. of first 3-tuple is < col no. of
            // second 3-tuple, then add info. as it is
            // to result
            if ( cola < colb )
            {
                * ( result + k * 3 + 0 ) = rowa ;
                * ( result + k * 3 + 1 ) = cola ;
                * ( result + k * 3 + 2 ) = vala ;
                i++ ;
            }

            // if col no. of first 3-tuple is > col no. of
            // second 3-tuple, then add info. as it is
            // to result
            if ( cola > colb )
            {
                * ( result + k * 3 + 0 ) = rowb ;
                * ( result + k * 3 + 1 ) = colb ;
                * ( result + k * 3 + 2 ) = valb ;
                j++ ;
            }
```

```
            k++ ;
        }

        // if row no. of first 3-tuple is < row no. of
        // second 3-tuple, then add info. as it is
        // to result

        if ( rowa < rowb )
        {
            * ( result + k * 3 + 0 ) = rowa ;
            * ( result + k * 3 + 1 ) = cola ;
            * ( result + k * 3 + 2 ) = vala ;
            i++ ;
            k++ ;
        }

        // if row no. of first 3-tuple is > row no. of
        // second 3-tuple, then add info. as it is
        // to result

        if ( rowa > rowb )
        {
            * ( result + k * 3 + 0 ) = rowb ;
            * ( result + k * 3 + 1 ) = colb ;
            * ( result + k * 3 + 2 ) = valb ;
            j++ ;
            k++ ;
        }
        elem++ ;
    }

    // add info about the total no. of rows, cols, and non-zero values
    // that the resultant array contains to the result
    * ( result + 0 ) = MAX1 ;
    * ( result + 1 ) = MAX2 ;
    * ( result + 2 ) = max ;
}

// displays the contents of the matrix
void sparse :: display_result( )
{
```

```
    // traverses the entire matrix
    for ( int i = 0 ; i < ( * ( result + 0 + 2 ) + 1 ) * 3 ; i++ )
    {
        // positions the cursor to the new line for every new row
        if ( i % 3 == 0 )
            cout << endl ;
        cout << * ( result + i ) << " " ;
    }
}

// deallocates memory
sparse :: ~sparse( )
{
    if ( sp != NULL )
        delete sp ;
    if ( result != NULL )
        delete result ;
}

int main( )
{
    sparse s1, s2 ;
    s1.create_array( ) ;
    s2.create_tuple ( s1 ) ;
    s2.display_tuple( ) ;
    sparse s3, s4 ;
    s3.create_array( ) ;
    s4.create_tuple ( s3 ) ;
    s4.display_tuple( ) ;
    sparse s5 ;
    s5.addmat ( s2, s4 ) ;
    cout << endl << "Result of addition of two matrices: " << endl ;
    s5.display_result( ) ;
    return 0 ;
}
```

Output:
Enter element no. 0: 1
Enter element no. 1: 0
Enter element no. 2: 2
Enter element no. 3: 0

Enter element no. 4: 3
Enter element no. 5: 0
Enter element no. 6: 4
Enter element no. 7: 0
Enter element no. 8: 0

Elements in a 3-tuple:
3 3 4
0 0 1
0 2 2
1 1 3
2 0 4

Enter element no. 0: 0
Enter element no. 1: 0
Enter element no. 2: 0
Enter element no. 3: 1
Enter element no. 4: 0
Enter element no. 5: 2
Enter element no. 6: 0
Enter element no. 7: 9
Enter element no. 8: 0

Elements in a 3-tuple:
3 3 3
1 0 1
1 2 2
2 1 9

Result of addition of two matrices:
3 3 7
0 0 1
0 2 2
1 0 1
1 1 3
1 2 2
2 0 4
2 1 9

The function **addmat( )** carries out addition of two sparse matrices. In this function firstly we have obtained the total number of non-zero elements that the target 3-tuple would hold. This has been achieved through the following statements:

amax = * (s1.sp + 2) ;
bmax = * (s2.sp + 2) ;
max = amax + bmax ;

Then we have allocated memory for the target 3-tuple that would store the result obtained from addition. Through a **while** loop we have carried out the addition operation. The variables **i** and **j** are used as counters for first 3-tuple (pointed to by **s1.sp**) and second 3-tuple (pointed to by **s2.sp**) respectively. Then we have retrieved the row number, column number and the non-zero value of ith and j^{th} non-zero element respectively. The following cases are considered while performing addition.

(a) If the row numbers as well as column numbers of the non-zero values retrieved from first and second 3-tuple (pointed to by s1.sp and s2.sp respectively) are same then we have added two non-zero values **vala** and **valb**. The row number **rowa**, column number **cola** and **vala + valb** is then copied to the target 3-tuple poited to by **result**.

(b) If column number of first 3-tuple is less than the column number of second 3-tuple, then we have added the information about the ith non-zero value of first 3-tuple to the target 3-tuple.

(c) If column number of first 3-tuple is greater than the column number of second 3-tuple, then we have added the information about the jth non-zero value of second 3-tuple to the target 3-tuple.

(d) If row number of first 3-tuple is less than the row number of second 3-tuple, then we have added the information about the ith non-zero value of first 3-tuple to the target 3-tuple.

(e) If row number of first 3-tuple is greater than the row number of second 3-tuple, then we have added the information about the jth non-zero value of second 3-tuple to the target 3-tuple.

Finally, the total number of rows, columns and non-zero values that the target 3-tuple holds is stored in the zeroth row of the target 3-tuple (pointed to by **result**). The function **display_result( )** displays result of the addition operation.

Linked Representation of a Sparse Matrix

Representing a sparse matrix as an array of 3-tuples suffers from one important limitation. When we carry out addition or multiplication it is not possible to predict beforehand how many elements in the resultant matrix would be non-zero. As a result, it is not possible to predict the size of the resultant matrix beforehand. Instead of an array we can represent the sparse matrix in the form of a linked list.

In the linked list representation a separate list is maintained for each column as well as each row of the matrix, i.e. if the matrix is of size 3 x 3, then there would be 3 lists for 3 columns and 3 lists for 3 rows. A node in a list stores the information about the non-zero element of the sparse matrix. The head node for a column list stores the column number, a pointer to the node, which comes first in the column, and a pointer to the next column head node. Thus the structure for column head node would be as shown below:

```
struct cheadnode
{
    struct node *down ;
    int colno ;
    cheadnode *next ;
}
```

A head node for a row list stores, a pointer to the node, which comes first in the row list, and a pointer to the next row head node. The structure for row head node would be as shown below:

```
structure rheadnode
{
    rheadnode *next ;
    int rowno ;
    struct node *right ;
}
```

A node on the other hand stores the row number, column number and the value of the non-zero element of the sparse matrix. It also stores a pointer to the node that is immediately to the right of the node in the row list as well as a pointer to the node that is immediately below the node in the column list. The structure for a node would be as shown below:

```
struct node
{
    int row, col, val ;
    node *down ;
    node *right ;
} ;
```

In addition to this a special node is used to store the total number of rows, total number of columns, a pointer to the first row head node and a pointer to the first column head node. The information stored in this special node is used for traversing the list. The structure of this special node would be as shown below:

```
struct spmat
{
    rheadnode *firstrow ;
    int noofrows, noofcols ;
    cheadnode *firstcol ;
} ;
```

If a particular column list is empty then the field **down** of the column head node would be NULL. Similarly if a row list is empty then the field **right** of the row head node would be empty. If a node is the last node in a particular column list or a particular row list then the field **down** or the field **right** of the node would be NULL.

Figure 4-2 gives pictorial representation of linked list of a sparse matrix of size 3 x 3.

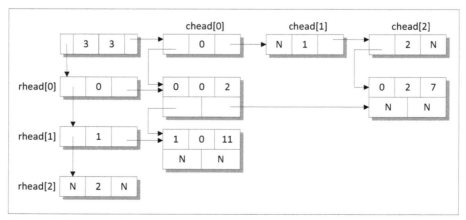

Figure 4-2. *Linked Representation of a sparse matrix.*

Other Forms of a Sparse Matrix

A square sparse matrix can be of following types:

Diagonal	Where the non-zero elements are stored on the leading diagonal of the matrix.
Tridiagonal	Where the non-zero elements are placed below or above the leading diagonal.
Lower Triangular	Where the non-zero elements are placed below the leading diagonal.
Upper Triangular	Where the non-zero elements are placed above the leading diagonal.

Figure 4-3 illustrates these four matrices.

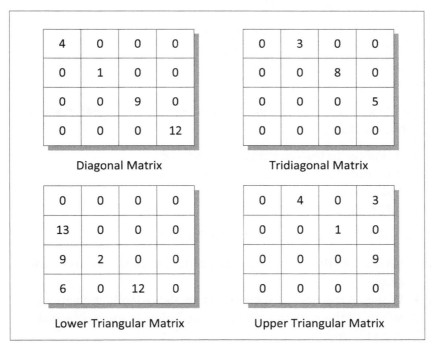

Figure 4-3. *Different forms of Sparse matrices.*

Chapter Bullets

Summary of chapter

(a) If many elements from a matrix have a value 0 then the matrix is known as a sparse matrix.

(b) A common way of representing non-zero elements of a sparse matrix is the 3-tuple form.

(c) Sparse matrix can be represented using either an array or a linked list.

(d) A square spare matrix may take the form of a Diagonal, Tridiagonal, Lower Triangular or Upper Triangular matrix.

Check Your Progress

Exercise - Level I

[A] Pick up the correct alternative for each of the following questions:

(a) A matrix is called sparse when

   (1) Most of its elements are non-zero
   (2) Most of its elements are zero
   (3) All of its elements are non-zero
   (4) None of the above

(b) In the linked representation of a sparse matrix the head node for a column list stores

   (1) A pointer to the next column head node
   (2) A pointer to the first node in column list
   (3) Column number
   (4) All of the above

(c) A sparse matrix can be lower-triangular matrix

   (1) When all the non-zero elements lie only on the leading diagonal.
   (2) When all the non-zero elements lie above leading diagonal.
   (3) When all the non-zero elements lie below leading diagonal.
   (4) Both (3) and (4)

Sharpen Your Skills

Exercise - Level II

[B] Answer the following:

(a) Write a program to build a sparse matrix as an array. Write functions to check if the sparse matrix is a square, diagonal, lower triangular, upper triangular or tridiagonal matrix.

(b) Write a program to subtract two sparse matrices implemented as an array.

(c) Write a program to build a spare matrix as a linked list. The program should provide functions for following operations:

    (i)   Store an element when the row number, column number and the value is provided.
    (ii) Retrieve an element for given row and column of the matrix.
    (iii) Add two sparse matrices
    (iv) Subtract two sparse matrices

Coding Interview Questions

Exercise Level III

Write a program that carries out multiplication of two sparse matrices through their 3-tuple form and stores the result in another sparse matrix in 3-tuple form.

Case Scenario Exercise

Linked representation of Sparse Matrix

Write a program that stores sparse matrix in the linked list form. The skeleton code for this program is given below. You are required to define different functions declared in the class **sparse** and the call these functions from **main( )**.

```
#include <iostream>
using namespace std ;
const int MAX1 = 3 ;
const int MAX2 = 3 ;
// structure for col head node
struct cheadnode
{
    struct node *down ;
    int colno ;
```

```
        cheadnode *next ;
} ;
// structure for row head node
struct rheadnode
{
    rheadnode *next ;
    int rowno ;
    struct node * right ;
} ;
// structure for node to store element
struct node
{
    int row, col, val ;
    node *down, *right ;
} ;
// structure for special head node
struct spmat
{
    rheadnode *firstrow ;
    int noofrows, noofcols ;
    cheadnode *firstcol ;
} ;
class sparse
{
    private :
        int *sp ;
        int row  ;
        spmat *smat ;
        cheadnode *chead[ MAX2 ] ;
        rheadnode *rhead[ MAX1 ] ;
        node *nd ;
    public :
        sparse( ) ;
        void create_array( ) ;
        void display( ) ;  int count( ) ;
        void create_triplet ( sparse &s ) ;
        void create_llist( ) ;
        void insert ( spmat *smat, int r, int c, int v ) ;
        void show_llist( ) ;
        ~sparse( ) ;
} ;
```

05
Chapter

—

Stacks
Of Wads Of Notes

Why This Chapter Matters?

Be it items in a store, books in a library, or notes in a
bank, the moment they become more than handful
we start stacking them neatly. Similarly, while
maintaining data in an orderly fashion it is placed in
a stack. Stack data structure is used widely for
storing variables, managing function calls,
evaluating arithmetic expressions, etc. Hence it is
important to understand this data structure
thoroughly.

S tack is a data structure in which addition of new element or deletion of an existing element always takes place at the same end. This end is known as **top** of stack. This situation can be compared to a stack of plates in a cafeteria where every new plate added to the stack is added at the **top**. Similarly, every new plate taken off the stack is also from the **top** of the stack. When an item is added to a stack, the operation is called **push**, and when an item is removed from the stack the operation is called **pop**. These operations are shown in Figure 5-1. Because of the nature of push and pop operations Stack is also called last-in-first-out (LIFO) list.

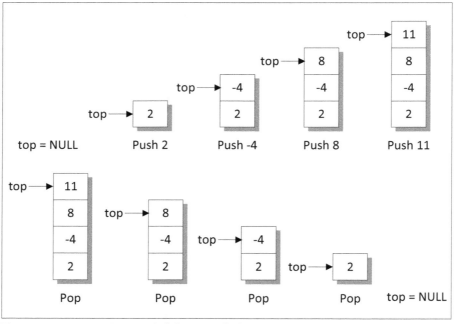

Figure 5-1. *Insertion and deletion of elements in a Stack.*

A stack data structure can be maintained as an array or as a linked list. The following sections discuss these implementations.

Stack as an Array

Stack contains an ordered collection of elements. An array is used to store ordered list of elements. Hence, a stack can be implemented using an array. However, we are required to declare the size of the array before using it. So when we use it to store elements of a stack the stack can grow or shrink within the memory reserved for the array. Let us now see a program that implements a stack using an array.

Honest Solid Code

{C++}

Program 5-1. Stack as an array

```cpp
#include <iostream>
using namespace std ;
const int MAX = 10 ;

class stack
{
    private :
        int arr[ MAX ] ;
        int top ;
    public :
        stack( ) ;
        void push ( int item ) ;
        int pop( ) ;
} ;

// initialises data member
stack :: stack( )
{
    top = -1 ;
}

// adds an element to the stack
void stack :: push ( int item )
{
    if ( top == MAX - 1 )
    {
        cout << "Stack is full" << endl ;
        return ;
    }
    top++ ;
    arr[ top ] = item ;
}

// extracts an element from the stack
int stack :: pop( )
{
```

```cpp
    if ( top == -1 )
    {
        cout << "Stack is empty" << endl ;
        return NULL ;
    }
    int data = arr[ top ] ;
    top-- ;
    return data ;
}

int main( )
{
    stack s ;

    s.push ( 2 ) ;
    s.push ( -4 ) ;
    s.push ( 8 ) ;
    s.push ( 11 ) ;

    int n = s.pop( ) ;
    if ( n != NULL )
        cout << "Item popped: " << n << endl ;

    n = s.pop( ) ;
    if ( n != NULL )
        cout << "Item popped: " << n << endl ;

    n = s.pop( ) ;
    if ( n != NULL )
        cout << "Item popped: " << n << endl ;

    n = s.pop( ) ;
    if ( n != NULL )
        cout << "Item popped: " << n << endl ;

    n = s.pop( ) ;
    if ( n != NULL )
        cout << "Item popped: " << n << endl ;

    return 0 ;
}
```

Output:

Item popped: 11
Item popped: 8
Item popped: -4
Item popped: 2
Stack is empty

In this program we have defined a class called **stack** containing **push( )** and **pop( )** functions. These functions are respectively used to add and delete items from the top of the stack. The actual storage of stack elements is done in an array **arr**. The data member **top** is an index into this array. It contains a value where the addition or deletion is going to take place in the array, and thereby in the stack. To indicate that the stack is empty to begin with, the variable **top** is set with a value -1 in the constructor function.

Every time an element is added to stack, it is verified whether such an addition is possible at all. If it is not, then the message 'Stack is full' is displayed. Since we have declared the array to hold 10 elements, the stack would be considered full if the value of **top** becomes equal to 9.

In **main( )** we have called **push( )** function to add 4 elements to the stack. Then we have removed these elements from the stack by calling the **pop( )** function. When we call **pop( )** for the 5th time, there are no elements present in the stack and top has a value -1 in it. Hence the 'Stack is empty' gets displayed.

Stack as a Linked List

In the earlier section we had used arrays to store the elements that get added to the stack. However, when implemented as an array it suffers from the basic limitation of an array—that its size cannot be increased or decreased once it is declared. As a result, one ends up reserving either too much memory or too less memory for an array and in turn for a stack. This problem can be overcome if we implement a stack using a linked list.

Each node in the linked list contains the data and a pointer that gives location of the next node in the list. The pointer to the beginning of the list serves the purpose of the top of the stack. Figure 5-2 shows the linked list representation of a stack.

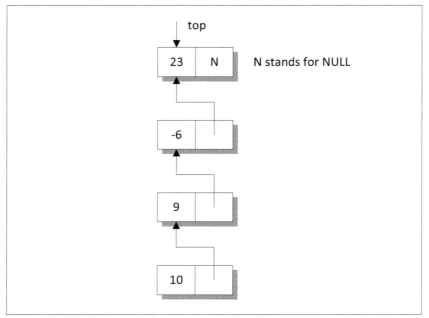

Figure 5-2. *Representation of stack as a linked list.*

Let us now see a program that implements stack as a linked list.

Honest Solid Code   {C++}

Program 5-2. Stack as a linked list

```cpp
#include <iostream>
using namespace std ;

class stack
{
    private :
        struct node
        {
            int data ;
            node *link ;
        } *top ;
    public :
        stack( ) ;
        void push ( int item ) ;
        int pop( ) ;
        ~stack( ) ;
```

```
} ;

// initialises data member
stack :: stack( )
{
    top = NULL ;
}

// adds a new node to the stack as linked list
void stack :: push ( int item )
{
    node *temp ;
    temp = new node ;

    if ( temp == NULL )
        cout << "Stack is full" << endl ;

    temp -> data = item ;
    temp -> link = top ;
    top = temp ;
}

// pops an element from the stack
int stack :: pop( )
{
    if ( top == NULL )
    {
        cout << "Stack is empty" << endl ;
        return NULL ;
    }

    node *temp ;
    int item ;

    temp = top ;
    item = temp -> data ;
    top = top -> link ;

    delete temp ;
    return item ;
}
```

```
// deallocates memory
stack :: ~stack( )
{
    if ( top == NULL )
        return ;

    node *temp ;
    while ( top != NULL )
    {
        temp = top ;
        top = top -> link ;
        delete temp ;
    }
}

int main( )
{
    stack s ;

    s.push ( 14 ) ;
    s.push ( -3 ) ;
    s.push ( 18 ) ;
    s.push ( 29 ) ;
    s.push ( 31 ) ;
    s.push ( 16 ) ;

    int n = s.pop( ) ;

    if ( n != NULL )
        cout << "Item popped: " << n << endl ;

    n = s.pop( ) ;
    if ( n != NULL )
        cout << "Item popped: " << n << endl ;

    n = s.pop( ) ;
    if ( n != NULL )
        cout << "Item popped: " << n << endl ;

    return 0 ;
```

}

Output:

Item popped: 16
Item popped: 31
Item popped: 29

Here we have designed a class called **stack**. Its data member **top** is a pointer to the structure **node**. Initially, **top** is set to **NULL** in the constructor to indicate that the stack is empty. In every call to the function **push( )** we are creating a new node dynamically. As long as there is enough memory available for dynamic allocation **temp** would never become **NULL**. If value of **temp** happens to be **NULL** then that would be a stage where stack would become full.

After, creating a new node, the data member **top** should point to the newly created item of the list. Hence we have assigned the address of this new node to **top**.

In the **pop( )** function, first we are checking whether or not a stack is empty. If so, then a message 'Stack is empty' gets displayed. If the stack is not empty then the topmost item gets removed from the list.

Applications of Stacks

Stacks are often used is in evaluation of arithmetic expression. An arithmetic expression consists of operands and operators. The operands can be constant or variables. The operators used in an arithmetic expression can be +, -, * and /.

While writing an arithmetic expression, the operator is placed between two operands as shown in the examples below.

A + B * C
A * B - C
A + B / C - D
A $ B + C

This way of representing arithmetic expressions is called **infix** notation. While evaluating an infix expression usually the following operator precedence is used:

- Highest priority: Exponentiation ($)
- Next highest priority: Multiplication (*) and Division (/)

   – Lowest priority: Addition (+) and Subtraction (-)

If we wish to override these priorities we can do so by using a pair of parentheses as shown below.

(A + B) * C
A * (B - C)
(A + B) / (C - D)

The expressions within a pair of parentheses are always evaluated earlier than other operations.

To make evaluation of an arithmetic expression easy, a polish mathematician Jan Lukasiewicz suggested a notation called **Polish** notation. As per this notation, an expression in **infix** form can be converted to either **prefix** or **postfix** form and then evaluated. In prefix notation the operator comes before the operands. In postfix notation, the operator follows the two operands. These forms are shown below.

A + B   - Infix form
+ A B   - Prefix form
A B +   - Postfix form

The prefix and postfix expressions have three features:

– The operands maintain the same order as in the equivalent infix expression
– Parentheses are not needed to designate the expression unambiguously.
– While evaluating the expression the priority of the operators is irrelevant.

The stack data structure is used while carrying out the conversion of an expression given in one form to another.

Infix to Postfix Conversion

Let us now see a program that converts an arithmetic expression given in an infix form to a postfix form.

Honest Solid Code   {C++}

Program 5-3. Infix to Postfix conversion

```cpp
#include <iostream>
#include <string.h>
#include <ctype.h>
using namespace std ;
const int MAX = 50 ;

class infix
{
    private :

        char target[ MAX ], stack[ MAX ] ;
        char *s, *t ;
        int top ;

    public :

        infix( ) ;
        void setexpr ( char *str ) ;
        void push ( char c ) ;
        char pop( ) ;
        void convert( ) ;
        int priority ( char c ) ;
        void show( ) ;
} ;

// initialises data members
infix :: infix( )
{
    top = -1 ;
    strcpy ( target, "" ) ;
    strcpy ( stack, "" ) ;
    t = target ;
    s = "" ;
}

// sets s to point to given expr.
void infix :: setexpr ( char *str )
{
    s = str ;
}
```

```
// adds an operator to the stack
void infix :: push ( char c )
{
    if ( top == MAX )
        cout << "Stack is full" << endl ;
    else
    {
        top++ ;
        stack[ top ] = c ;
    }
}

// pops an operator from the stack
char infix :: pop( )
{
    if ( top == -1 )
    {
        cout << "Stack is empty" << endl ;
        return -1 ;
    }
    else
    {
        char item = stack[ top ] ;
        top-- ;
        return item ;
    }
}

// converts the given expr. from infix to postfix form
void infix :: convert( )
{
    while ( *s )
    {
        if ( *s == ' ' || *s == '\t' )
        {
            s++ ;
            continue ;
        }

        if ( isdigit ( *s ) || isalpha ( *s ) )
        {
```

```
            while ( isdigit ( *s ) || isalpha ( *s ) )
            {
                *t = *s ;
                s++ ;
                t++ ;
            }
        }

    if ( *s == '(' )
    {
        push ( *s ) ;
        s++ ;
    }

    char opr ;
    if ( *s == '*' || *s == '+' || *s == '/' || *s == '%' || *s == '-' ||
        *s == '$' )
    {
        if ( top != -1 )
        {
            opr = pop( ) ;
            while ( priority ( opr ) >= priority ( *s ) )
            {
                *t = opr ;
                t++ ;
                opr = pop( ) ;
            }
            push ( opr ) ;
            push ( *s ) ;
        }
        else
            push ( *s ) ;
        s++ ;
    }

    if ( *s == ')' )
    {
        opr = pop( ) ;
        while ( ( opr ) != '(' )
        {
            *t = opr ;
```

```
                t++ ;
                opr =  pop( ) ;
            }
            s++ ;
        }
    }

    while ( top != -1 )
    {
        char opr = pop( ) ;
        *t = opr ;
        t++ ;
    }
    *t = '\0' ;
}

// returns the priority of an operator
int infix :: priority ( char c )
{
    if ( c == '$' )
        return 3 ;
    if ( c == '*' || c == '/' || c == '%' )
        return 2 ;
    else
    {
        if ( c == '+' || c == '-' )
            return 1 ;
        else
            return 0 ;
    }
}

// displays the postfix form of given expr.
void infix :: show( )
{
    cout << target << endl ;
}

int main( )
{
    char expr[ MAX ] ;
```

```
    infix q ;

    cout << "Enter an expression in Infix form: " << endl ;
    cin.getline ( expr, MAX ) ;

    q.setexpr ( expr ) ;
    q.convert( ) ;

    cout << "The Postfix expression is: " << endl ;
    q.show( ) ;

    return 0 ;
}
```

Output:

Enter an expression in infix form:
4 $ 2 * 3 - 3 + 8 / 4 / (1 + 1)
Stack is empty
The postfix expression is:
42$3*3-84/11+/+

This program contains a class called **infix**. The data members **target** and **stack** are used to store the postfix string and to maintain the stack respectively. The **char** pointers **s** and **t** are used to store intermediate results while converting an infix expression to a postfix form. The data member **top** points to the top of the stack.

During program execution when user enters an arithmetic expression the function **setexpr( )** assigns the base address of the string to **char** pointer **s**.

Next, the function **convert( )** gets called. This function converts the given infix expression to postfix expression. This function scans every character of the string in a **while** loop and performs one of the following operation depending on the type of character scanned.

(a) If the character scanned happens to be a space then that character is skipped.

(b) If character scanned is a digit or an alphabet, it is added to the target string pointed to by **t**.

(c) If the character scanned is a closing parenthesis then it is pushed to the stack by calling **push( )** function.

(d) If the character scanned is an operator, then firstly, the topmost element from the stack is retrieved. Through a **while** loop, the priorities of the character scanned (i.e. ***s**) and the character popped **opr** are compared. Then following steps are performed:

(i) If **opr** has higher or same priority as the character scanned, then **opr** is added to the target string.

(ii) If **opr** has lower precedence than the character scanned, then the loop is terminated. **opr** is pushed back to the stack. Then, the character scanned (***s**) is also pushed to the stack.

(e) If the character scanned is an opening parenthesis, then the operators present in the stack are popped through a loop. The loop continues till it does not encounter a closing parenthesis. The popped operators are added to the target string pointed to by **t**.

In the **convert( )** function we have called functions **push( )**, **pop( )**, **priority( )**. The **push( )** function adds a character to the stack, whereas the **pop( )** function removes the topmost item from the stack. The **priority( )** function returns the priority of operators used in the infix expression. $ (exponentiation) has the highest precedence, followed by *, / and +, -. The function returns integer 3 for $, 2 for * or /, 1 for + or - and 0 for any other character.

The **while** loop in **convert( )** gets terminated if the string **s** is exhausted. By then some operators may still be in the stack. These operators should get added to the postfix string. This is done once the control reaches outside the **while** loop in the **convert( )** function. Lastly, the converted expression is displayed using the **show( )** function.

The steps performed in the conversion of a sample infix expression 4 $ 2 * 3 - 3 + 8 / 4 / (1 + 1) to a postfix expression are shown in Table 5-1.

Infix Expression: 4 $ 2 * 3 - 3 + 8 / 4 / (1 + 1)		
Char Scanned	**Stack Contents**	**Postfix Expression**
4	Empty	4
$	$	4
2	$	4 2
*	*	4 2 $
3	*	4 2 $ 3
-	-	4 2 $ 3 *
3	-	4 2 $ 3 * 3
+	+	4 2 $ 3 * 3 -
8	+	4 2 $ 3 * 3 - 8
/	+ /	4 2 $ 3 * 3 - 8
4	+ /	4 2 $ 3 * 3 − 8 4
/	+ /	4 2 $ 3 * 3 − 8 4 /
(	+ / (	4 2 $ 3 * 3 − 8 4 /
1	+ / (	4 2 $ 3 * 3 − 8 4 / 1
+	+ / (+	4 2 $ 3 * 3 − 8 4 / 1
1	+ / (+	4 2 $ 3 * 3 − 8 4 / 1 1
)	+ /	4 2 $ 3 * 3 − 8 4 / 1 1 +
	Empty	4 2 $ 3 * 3 − 8 4 / 1 1 + / +

Table 5-1. *Conversion of Infix to Postfix form.*

Postfix to Prefix Conversion

Let us now see a program that converts an expression in postfix form to a prefix form.

Honest Solid Code   {C++}

Program 5-4. Postfix to Prefix conversion

```cpp
#include <iostream>
#include <string.h>
using namespace std ;
const int MAX = 50 ;
```

```
class postfix
{
    private :

        char stack[ MAX ][ MAX ], target[ MAX ] ;
        char temp1[ 2 ], temp2[ 2 ] ;
        char str1[ MAX ], str2[ MAX ], str3[ MAX ] ;
        int i, top ;

    public :

        postfix( ) ;
        void setexpr ( char *c ) ;
        void push ( char *str ) ;
        void pop ( char *a ) ;
        void convert( ) ;
        void show( ) ;
} ;

// initialises data members
postfix :: postfix( )
{
    i = 0 ;
    top = -1 ;
    strcpy ( target, "" ) ;
}

// copies given expression to target string
void postfix :: setexpr ( char *c )
{
    strcpy ( target, c ) ;
}

// adds an operator to the stack
void postfix :: push ( char *str )
{
    if ( top == MAX - 1 )
        cout << endl << "Stack is full" ;
    else
    {
```

```
        top++ ;
        strcpy ( stack[ top ], str ) ;
    }
}

// pops an element from the stack
void postfix :: pop ( char *a )
{
    if ( top == -1 )
        cout << "Stack  is empty" << endl ;
    else
    {
        strcpy ( a, stack[ top ] ) ;
        top-- ;
    }
}

// converts given expression to prefix form
void postfix :: convert( )
{
    while ( target[ i ] != '\0' )
    {
        // skip whitespace, if any
        if ( target[ i ] == ' ')
            i++ ;
        if( target[ i ] == '%' || target[ i ] == '*' ||
            target[ i ] == '-' || target[ i ] == '+' ||
            target[ i ] == '/' || target[ i ] == '$' )
        {
            pop ( str2 ) ;
            pop ( str3 ) ;
            temp1[ 0 ] = target[ i ] ;
            temp1[ 1 ] = '\0' ;
            strcpy ( str1, temp1 ) ;
            strcat ( str1, str3 ) ;
            strcat ( str1, str2 ) ;
            push ( str1 ) ;
        }
        else
        {
            temp1[ 0 ] = target[ i ] ;
```

```
                temp1[ 1 ] = '\0' ;
                strcpy ( temp2, temp1 ) ;
                push ( temp2 ) ;
        }
                i++ ;
        }
}

// displays the prefix form of expression
void postfix :: show( )
{
    char *temp  = stack[ 0 ] ;
    while ( *temp )
    {
        cout << *temp << " " ;
        temp++ ;
    }
    cout << endl ;
}

int main( )
{
    char expr[ MAX ] ;

    cout << "Enter an expression in Postfix form: " << endl ;
    cin.getline ( expr, MAX ) ;

    postfix q ;
    q.setexpr ( expr ) ;
    q.convert( ) ;

    cout << "The Prefix expression is: " << endl ;
    q.show( ) ;

    return 0 ;
}
```

Output:

Enter an expression in postfix form:
4 2 $ 3 * 3 - 8 4 / 1 1 + / +
The Prefix expression is:

+ - * $ 4 2 3 3 / / 8 4 + 1 1

In this program the class **postfix** contains character arrays like **temp1**, **temp2, str1, str2, str3** to store the intermediate results. The character arrays **stack** and **target** are used to maintain the stack and to store the final string in the prefix form respectively.

In the **convert( )** function the string containing expression in postfix form is scanned through a **while** loop till the string **target** is not exhausted. Following steps are performed depending on the type of character scanned.

(a) If the character scanned is a space then that character is skipped.

(b) If the character scanned contains a digit or an alphabet, it is pushed to the stack by calling **push( )** function.

(c) If the character scanned contains an operator, then the topmost two elements are popped from the stack. These two elements are then stored in the array **temp1**. A temporary string **temp2** containing the operator and the two operands is formed. This temporary string is then pushed on the stack.

The converted prefix form is stored at the 0th position in the stack. Finally, the **show( )** function displays this prefix form. The steps performed in the conversion of a sample postfix expression 4 2 $ 3 * 3 - 8 4 / 1 1 + / + to its equivalent prefix expression is shown in Table 5-2.

Postfix Expression: 4 2 $ 3 * 3 - 8 4 / 1 1 + / +	
Char. Scanned	**Stack Contents**
4	4
2	4 2
$	$ 4 2
3	$ 4 2 3
*	* $ 4 2 3
3	* $ 4 2 3 , 3
-	- * $ 4 2 3 3
8	- * $ 4 2 3 3 , 8
4	- * $ 4 2 3 3 , 8 , 4
/	- * $ 4 2 3 3 , / 8 4
1	- * $ 4 2 3 3 , / 8 4 , 1
1	- * $ 4 2 3 3 , / 8 4 , 1 , 1
+	- * $ 4 2 3 3 , / 8 4 , + 1 1
/	- * $ 4 2 3 3 , / / 8 4 + 1 1
+	+ - $ 4 2 3 3 / / 8 4 + 1 1

Table 5-2. *Conversion of Infix to Postfix form.*

Other Inter-Conversions

We have seen conversion of infix to postfix form and postfix to prefix form. It is also possible to carry out other conversions as well. Figure 5-3 summarizes the operations to be performed to carry out these inter-conversions.

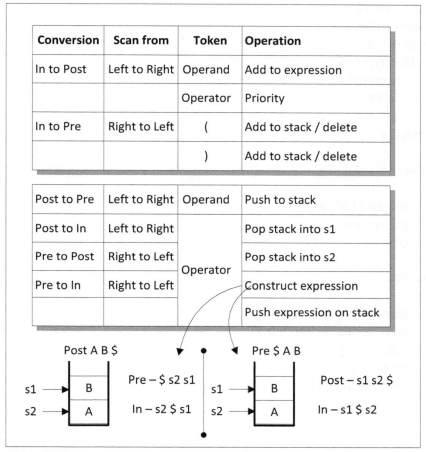

Figure 5-3. *Summary of inter-conversion of expressions.*

Evaluation of Postfix Expression

The virtue of postfix notation is that it enables easy evaluation of expressions. To begin with, the need for parentheses is eliminated. Secondly, the priority of the operators is no longer relevant. The expression can be evaluated by making a left to right scan, stacking operands, and evaluating operators using operands popped from the stack and finally placing the result onto the stack. This evaluation is much simpler than attempting a direct evaluation of infix notation. Let us now see a program to evaluate a postfix expression.

Honest Solid Code   {C++}

Program 5-5. Evaluation of Postfix expression

```
#include <iostream>
#include <stdlib.h>
#include <math.h>
#include <ctype.h>
using namespace std ;
const int MAX = 50 ;

class postfix
{
    private :

        int stack[ MAX ] ;
        int top, nn ;
        char *s ;

    public :

        postfix( ) ;
        void setexpr ( char *str ) ;
        void push ( int item ) ;
        int pop( ) ;
        void calculate( ) ;
        void show( ) ;
} ;

// initialises data members
postfix :: postfix( )
{
    top = -1 ;
}

// sets s to point to the given expr.
void postfix :: setexpr ( char *str )
{
    s = str ;
}

// adds digit to the stack
void postfix :: push ( int item )
{
    if ( top == MAX - 1 )
```

```
            cout << "Stack is full" << endl ;
        else
        {
            top++ ;
            stack[ top ] = item ;
        }
}

// pops digit from the stack
int postfix :: pop( )
{
    if ( top == -1 )
    {
        cout << "Stack is empty" << endl ;
            return NULL ;
    }
    int data = stack[ top ] ;
    top-- ;
    return data ;
}

// evaluates the postfix expression
void postfix :: calculate( )
{
    int n1, n2, n3 ;
    while ( *s )
    {
        // skip whitespace, if any
        if ( *s == ' ' || *s == '\t' )
        {
            s++ ;
            continue ;
        }

        // if digit is encountered
        if ( isdigit ( *s ) )
        {
            nn = *s - '0' ;
            push ( nn ) ;
        }
        else
```

```cpp
        {
            // if operator is encountered
            n1 = pop( ) ;
            n2 = pop( ) ;
            switch ( *s )
            {
                case '+' :
                    n3 = n2 + n1 ;
                    break ;
                case '-' :
                    n3 = n2 - n1 ;
                    break ;
                case '/' :
                    n3 = n2 / n1 ;
                    break ;
                case '*' :
                    n3 = n2 * n1 ;
                    break ;
                case '%' :
                    n3 = n2 % n1 ;
                    break ;
                case '$' :
                    n3 = ( int ) pow ( ( double ) n2 , ( double ) n1 ) ;
                    break ;
                default :
                    cout << "Unknown operator" << endl ;
                    exit ( 1 ) ;
            }
            push ( n3 ) ;
        }
        s++ ;
    }
}

// displays the result
void postfix :: show( )
{
    nn = pop ( ) ;
    cout << "Result is: " << nn << endl ;
}
```

```
int main( )
{
    char expr[ MAX ] ;

    cout << "Enter Postfix expression to be evaluated: " << endl ;
    cin.getline ( expr, MAX ) ;

    postfix q ;

    q.setexpr ( expr ) ;
    q.calculate( ) ;
    q.show( ) ;

    return 0 ;
}
```

Output:

Enter postfix expression to be evaluated:
4 2 $ 3 * 3 - 8 4 / 1 1 + / +
Result is: 46

In this program the class **postfix** contains an integer array **stack**, to store the intermediate results of the operations and **top** to store the position of the topmost element in the stack. The evaluation of the expression gets performed in the **calculate( )** function.

During execution the user enters an arithmetic expression in postfix form. In the **calculate( )** function, this expression gets scanned character by character. If the character scanned is a blank space, then it is skipped. If the character scanned is an operand, then first it is converted to a digit form (from string form), and then it is pushed onto the stack. If the character scanned is an operator, then the top two elements from the stack are popped, an arithmetic operation is performed between them and the result is then pushed back onto the **stack**. These steps are repeated as long as the string **s** is not exhausted. The **show( )** function displays the final result. These steps can be better understood if you go through the evaluation of a sample postfix expression shown in Table 5-3.

Postfix Expression: 4 2 $ 3 * 3 - 8 4 / 1 1 + / +	
Char. Scanned	**Stack Contents**
4	4
2	4, 2
$	16
3	16, 3
*	48
3	48, 3
-	45
8	45, 8
4	45, 8, 4
/	45, 2
1	45, 2, 1
1	45, 2, 1, 1
+	45, 2, 2
/	45, 1
+	46 (Result)

Table 5-3. *Evaluation of Postfix expression.*

Chapter Bullets

Summary of chapter

(a) Stack data structure is a LIFO list in which addition of new elements and deletion of existing elements takes place at the same end.

(b) Addition of a new element to a stack is called push operation.

(c) Deletion of an existing element from a stack is called pop operation.

(d) Stack data structure can be implemented using an array or a linked list.

(e) If stack is implemented as a linked list, push operation is like adding a new node at the beginning of the linked list.

(f) If stack is implemented as a linked list, pop operation is like deleting an existing node from the beginning of the linked list.

(g) Stack data structure has many applications like keeping track of function calls, storing local variable, evaluation of arithmetic expression, etc.

Check Your Progress

Exercise - Level I

[A] Fill in the blanks:

(a) A stack is a data structure in which addition of new element or deletion of an existing element always takes place at an end called _____.

(b) The data structure stack is also called _____ list.

(c) In _____ notation the operators precedes the two operands.

(d) In _____ notation the operator follows the two operands.

[B] Pick up the correct alternative for each of the following questions:

(a) Adding an element to the stack means
    (1) Placing an element at the front end
    (2) Placing an element at the top
    (3) Placing an element at the rear end
    (4) None of the above

(b) Pushing an element to a stack means
    (1) Removing an element from the stack
    (2) Searching a given element in the stack
    (3) Adding a new element to the stack
    (4) Sorting the elements in the stack

(c) Popping an element from the stack means
    (1) Removing an element from the stack
    (2) Searching a given element in the stack
    (3) Adding a new element to the stack
    (4) Sorting the elements in the stack

(d) The expression A B *
    (1) is an infix expression
    (2) is a postfix expression
    (3) is a prefix expression
    (4) is a stack expression

Sharpen Your Skills

Exercise - Level II

[C] Transform the following infix expressions into their equivalent postfix expressions:

(A - B) * (D / E)
(A + B ^ D) / (E - F) + G
A * (B + D) / E - F * (G + H / K)
(A + B) * (C - D) $ E * F
(A + B) * (C $ (D - E) + F) / G) $ (H - J)

[D] Transform the following infix expressions into their equivalent prefix expressions:

(A - B) * (D / E)
(A + B ^ D) / (E - F) + G
A * (B + D) / E - F * (G + H / K)

[E] Transform each of the following prefix expression to infix.

+ A - B C
+ + A - * $ B C D / + E F * G H I
+ - $ A B C * D ** E F G

[F] Transform each of the following postfix expression to infix.

A B C + -
A B - C + D E F - + $
A B C D E - + $ * E F * -

Coding Interview Questions

Exercise Level III

[G] Write programs for the following:

(a) Copying contents of one stack to another.

(b) To check whether in a string containing an arithmetic expression, the opening and closing parenthesis are well- formed or not.

Case Scenario Exercise

Prefix to postfix and infix forms

Write a program to convert an arithmetic expression in prefix form to equivalent infix and postfix forms. Refer Figure 5-4 for the steps to be carried out in each of these conversions.

06
Chapter

—

Queues
Await Your Turn

Why This Chapter Matters?

Whether it is a railway reservation counter, a movie theatre or print jobs submitted to a network printer there is only one way to bring order to chaos—form a queue. If you await your turn patiently, there is a more likelihood that you would get a better service. In a computer system too there are queues of tasks (programs) waiting for the printer, or for access to disk storage, or for usage of CPU, etc. Understand this chapter thoroughly to be able to implement queues.

Queue is a linear data structure that permits insertion of new element at one end and deletion of an element at the other end. The end at which the deletion of an element takes place is called **front**, and the end at which insertion of a new element takes place is called **rear**.

The first element that gets added into the queue is the first one to get removed from the list. Hence, queue is also referred to as first-in-first-out (FIFO) list. The name 'queue' comes from the everyday use of the term. Consider a queue of people waiting at a bus stop. Each new person who comes takes his or her place at the end of the line, and when the bus arrives, the people at the front of the line board first. The first person in the line is the first person to leave it. Figure 6-1 gives a pictorial representation of a queue.

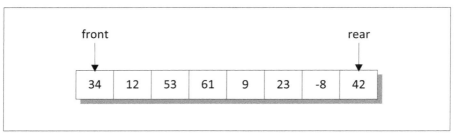

Figure 6-1. *Pictorial representation of a queue.*

In Figure 6-1, 34 is the first element and 42 is the last element added to the queue. Similarly, 34 will be the first element to get removed and 42 will be the last element to get removed from the queue.

Queue, being a linear data structure can be represented using either an array or a linked list. These implementations are discussed in following sections.

Queue as an Array

Representing a queue as an array would have the same problem that we discussed in case of stack in Chapter 5. An array can store a fixed number of elements. Queue, on the other hand keeps on changing as we remove elements from the front end or add new elements at the rear end. Declaring an array with a maximum size would solve this problem. The maximum size should be large enough for a queue to expand or shrink. Let us now see a program that implements queue as an array.

Honest Solid Code   {C++}

Program 6-1. Implementation of queue as an array

```cpp
#include <iostream>
using namespace std ;
const int MAX = 10 ;

class queue
{
    private :
        int arr[ MAX ] ;
        int front, rear ;
    public :
        queue( ) ;
        void addq ( int item ) ;
        int delq( ) ;
} ;

// initialises data members
queue :: queue( )
{
    front = -1 ;
    rear = -1 ;
}

// adds an element to the queue
void queue :: addq ( int item )
{
    if ( rear == MAX - 1 )
    {
        cout << "Queue is full" << endl ;
        return ;
    }

    rear++ ;
    arr[ rear ] = item ;

    if ( front == -1 )
        front = 0 ;
```

```
}

// removes an element from the queue
int queue :: delq( )
{
    int data ;

    if ( front == -1 )
    {
        cout << "Queue is Empty" << endl ;
        return NULL ;
    }
    data = arr[ front ] ;
    arr[ front ] = 0 ;
    if ( front == rear )
        front = rear = -1 ;
    else
        front++ ;

    return  data ;
}

int main( )
{
    queue q ;

    q.addq ( 34 ) ;
    q.addq ( 12 ) ;
    q.addq ( 53 ) ;
    q.addq ( 61 ) ;

    int n ;
    n = q.delq( ) ;
    if ( n != NULL )
        cout << "Item deleted: " << n << endl ;

    n = q.delq( ) ;
    if ( n != NULL )
        cout << "Item deleted: " << n << endl ;

    n = q.delq( ) ;
```

```
        if ( n != NULL )
            cout << "Item deleted: " << n << endl ;

        n = q.delq( ) ;
        if ( n != NULL )
            cout << "Item deleted: " << n << endl ;

        n = q.delq( ) ;
        if ( n != NULL )
            cout << "Item deleted: " << n << endl ;
}
```

Output:

Item deleted: 34
Item deleted: 12
Item deleted: 53
Item deleted: 61
Queue is Empty

Here we have designed a class called **queue**. It contains an array **arr** to store queue elements and variables **front** and **rear** to monitor the two ends of the queue. The initial values of **front** and **rear** are set to -1, through the constructor to mark the queue as empty. The functions **addq( )** and **delq( )** are used to perform addition and deletion operations on the queue.

In **addq( )** firstly it is ascertained whether an addition is possible or not. Since the array indexing begins with 0 the maximum number of elements that can be stored in the queue are **MAX** - 1. If these many elements are already present in the queue then it is reported to be full. If an element can be added to the queue then value of **rear** is incremented and the new item is stored in the array.

If the item being added to the queue is the first element (i.e. if variable **front** has a value -1) then as soon as the item is added to the queue **front** is set to 0 indicating that the queue is no longer empty.

The addition of an element to the queue is illustrated in Figure 6-2.

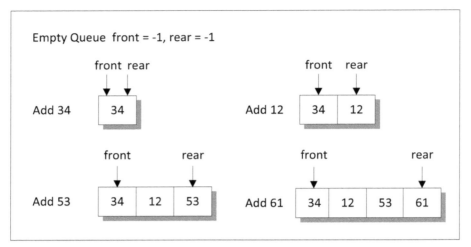

Figure 6-2. *Addition of an element to a queue.*

Let us now see how the **delq( )** function works. Before deleting an element from the queue it is first ascertained whether there are any elements available for deletion. If not, then the queue is reported as empty. Otherwise, an element is deleted form **arr[front]**.

Imagine a case where we add 10 elements to the queue. Value of **rear** would now be 9. Suppose we have not deleted any elements from the queue, then at this stage the value of **front** would be 0. Now suppose we go on deleting elements from the queue. When the tenth element is deleted the queue would fall empty. To make sure that another attempt to delete should be met with an 'empty queue' message, **front** and **rear** both are reset to -1 to indicate emptiness of the queue.

The deletion of elements from a queue is illustrated in Figure 6-3.

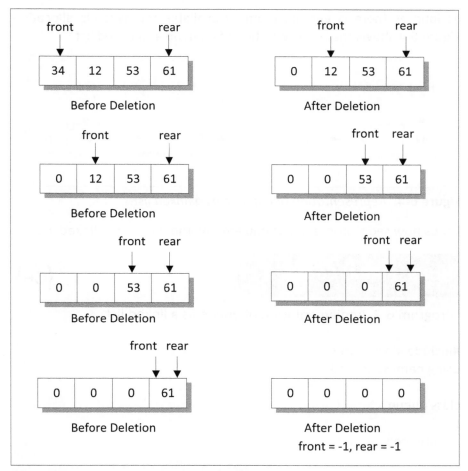

Figure 6-3. *Deletion of elements from a queue.*

Our program has got one limitation. Suppose we go on adding elements to the queue till the entire array gets filled. At this stage the value of **rear** would be **MAX** - 1. Now if we delete 5 elements from the queue, at the end of these deletions the value of **front** would be 5. If now we attempt to add a new element to the queue then it would be reported as full even though in reality the first five slots of the queue are empty. To overcome this situation we can implement a queue as a circular queue, which would be discussed later in this chapter.

Queue as a Linked-List

Queue can also be represented using a linked list. Linked lists do not have any restrictions on the number of elements it can hold. Space for the elements in a linked list is allocated dynamically, hence it can grow as long as there is enough memory available for dynamic allocation. Figure 6-4 shows the representation of a queue as a linked list.

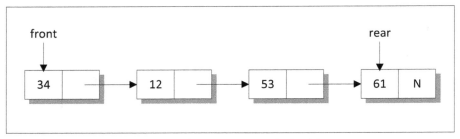

Figure 6-4. *Representation of a queue as a linked list.*

Let us now see a program that implements the queue as a linked list.

Honest Solid Code   {C++}

Program 6-2. Implementation of queue as a linked list

```cpp
#include <iostream>
using namespace std ;

class queue
{
    private :

        struct node
        {
            int data ;
            node *link ;
        } *front, *rear ;

    public :

        queue( ) ;
        void addq ( int item ) ;
        int delq( ) ;
        ~queue( ) ;
} ;

// initialises data member
queue :: queue( )
```

```
{
    front = rear = NULL ;
}

// adds an element to the queue
void queue :: addq ( int item )
{
    node *temp ;

    temp = new node ;
    if ( temp == NULL )
        cout << "Queue is full" << endl ;

    temp -> data = item ;
    temp -> link = NULL ;

    if ( front == NULL )
    {
        rear = front = temp ;
        return ;
    }

    rear -> link = temp ;
    rear = rear -> link ;
}

// removes an element from the queue
int queue :: delq( )
{
    if ( front == NULL )
    {
        cout << "Queue is empty" << endl ;
        return NULL ;
    }

    node *temp ;
    int item ;

    item = front  -> data ;
    temp = front ;
    front = front -> link ;
```

```
        delete temp ;
        return item ;
}

// deallocates memory
queue :: ~queue( )
{
    if ( front == NULL )
        return ;

    node *temp ;
    while ( front != NULL )
    {
        temp = front ;
        front = front -> link ;
        delete temp ;
    }
}

int main( )
{
    queue q ;

    q.addq ( 34 ) ;
    q.addq ( 12 ) ;
    q.addq ( 53 ) ;
    q.addq ( 61 ) ;

    int n = q.delq( ) ;
    if ( n != NULL )
        cout << "Item extracted: " << n << endl ;

    n = q.delq( ) ;
    if ( n != NULL )
        cout << "Item extracted: " << n << endl ;

    n = q.delq( ) ;
    if ( n != NULL )
        cout << "Item extracted: " << n << endl ;
}
```

Output:

Item deleted: 34
Item deleted: 12
Item deleted: 53

In this program the class **queue** contains two data members **front** and **rear**, both pointers to the structure **node**. To begin with, the queue is empty hence both **front** and **rear** are set to **NULL** in the constructor of the queue class.

The **addq( )** function adds a new element at the rear end of the list. If the element added is the first element, then both **front** and **rear** are made to point to the new node. However, if the element added is not the first element then only **rear** is made to point to the new node, whereas **front** continues to point to the first node in the list.

The **delq( )** function removes an element from the list which is at the front end of the list. Removal of an element from the list actually deletes the node to which **front** is pointing. After deletion of a node, **front** is made to point to the next node that comes in the list, whereas **rear** continues to point to the last node in the list.

When the program terminates, the object **q** dies. As a result, the destructor is called. In the destructor the memory allocated for the existing nodes in the list is de-allocated.

Circular Queue

The queue that we implemented using an array suffers from one limitation. In that implementation there is a possibility that the queue is reported as full (since **rear** has reached the end of the array), even though in actuality there might be empty slots at the beginning of the queue.

To overcome this limitation we can implement the queue as a circular queue. Here as we go on adding elements to the queue and reach the end of the array, the next element is stored in the first slot of the array (provided it is free).

More clearly, suppose an array **arr** of **n** elements is used to implement a circular queue. As we go on adding elements to the queue we will reach **arr[n-1]**. We cannot add any more elements to the queue as we have reached the end of the array. If some elements in the queue are deleted the slots at the beginning of the queue will fall vacant. If now any new elements are to be added to the queue, instead of reporting that the queue is full we fill the slots at the beginning of the array with new elements being added to the queue.

In short, just because we have reached the end of the array the queue would not be reported as full. The queue would be reported as full only when all the slots in the array stand occupied.

Let us now see a program that performs the addition and deletion operation on a circular queue.

Honest Solid Code

{C++}

Program 6-3. Implementation of circular queue

```cpp
#include <iostream>
using namespace std ;
const int MAX = 8 ;

class queue
{
    private :

        int arr[ MAX ] ;
        int front, rear ;

    public :

        queue( ) ;
        void addq ( int item ) ;
        int delq( ) ;
        void display( ) ;
} ;

// initialises data member
queue :: queue( )
{
    front = rear = -1 ;
    for ( int i = 0 ; i < MAX ; i++ )
        arr[ i ] = 0 ;
}
```

```
// adds an element to the queue
void queue :: addq ( int item )
{
    if ( ( rear == MAX - 1 && front == 0 ) || ( rear + 1 == front ) )
    {
        cout << "Queue is full" << endl ;
        return ;
    }

    if ( rear == MAX - 1 )
        rear = 0 ;
    else
        rear++ ;

    arr[ rear ] = item ;

    if ( front == -1 )
        front = 0 ;
}

// removes an element from the queue
int queue :: delq( )
{
    int data ;

    if ( front == -1 )
    {
        cout << "Queue is empty" << endl ;
        return NULL ;
    }

    data = arr[ front ] ;
    arr[ front ] = 0 ;

    if ( front == rear )
    {
        front = -1 ;
        rear = -1 ;
    }
    else
```

```
    {
        if ( front == MAX - 1 )
            front = 0 ;
        else
            front++ ;
    }
    return data ;
}

// displays element in a queue
void queue :: display( )
{
    for ( int i = 0 ; i < MAX ; i++ )
        cout << arr[ i ] << " " ;
    cout << endl ;
}

int main( )
{
    queue q ;

    q.addq ( 14 ) ;
    q.addq ( 22 ) ;
    q.addq ( 13 ) ;
    q.addq ( -6 ) ;
    q.addq ( 25 ) ;
    q.addq ( 21 ) ;
    q.addq ( 17 ) ;
    q.addq ( 18 ) ;

    cout << "Elements in the circular queue: " << endl ;
    q.display( ) ;

    int i = q.delq( ) ;
    cout << "Item deleted: " << i << endl ;

    i = q.delq( ) ;
    cout << "Item deleted: " << i << endl ;

    cout << "Elements in the circular queue after deletion: " << endl ;
    q.display( ) ;
```

```
        q.addq ( 9 );
        q.addq ( 20 );

        cout << "Elements in the circular queue after addition: " << endl ;
        q.display( ) ;
}
```

Output:

Elements in the circular queue:
14   22   13   -6   25   21   17   18
Item deleted: 14
Item deleted: 22
Elements in the circular queue after deletion:
0   0   13   -6   25   21   17   18
Elements in the circular queue after addition:
9   20   13   -6   25   21   17   18

In this program the class **queue** contains an array **arr** to store the elements of the circular queue. The functions **addq( )** and **delq( )** are used to add and remove the elements from the queue respectively. The function **display( )** displays the existing elements of the queue. The initial values of **front** and **rear** are set to -1, to mark the queue as empty.

In **main( )**, first we have called the **addq( )** function 8 times to insert elements in the circular queue. In this function, following cases are considered before adding an element to the queue.

(a)   First we have checked whether or not the array is full. The message 'Queue is full' gets displayed if **front** and **rear** are in adjacent locations with **rear** following the **front**.

(b)   If the value of **front** is -1 then it indicates that the queue is empty and the element to be added would be the first element in the queue. The values of **front** and **rear** in such a case are set to 0 and the new element gets placed at the 0th position.

(c)   It may also happen that some of the positions at the front end of the array are vacant. This happens if we have deleted some elements from the queue, when the value of **rear** is **MAX** - 1 and the value of **front** is greater than 0. In such a case the value of **rear** is set to 0 and the element to be added is added at this position.

(d) The element is added at the rear position in case the value of **front** is either equal to or greater than 0 and the value of **rear** is less than **MAX** - 1.

Thus, after adding 8 elements the value of **front** and **rear** become 0 and 7 respectively. The **display( )** function displays the elements in the queue. Figure 6-5 shows the circular queue after adding 8 elements.

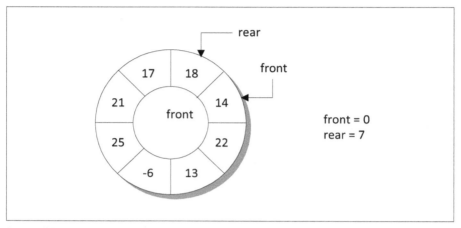

Figure 6-5. *Circular queue after addition of 8 elements.*

Next we have called **delq( )** function twice to remove 2 elements from the queue. The following conditions are checked while deleting an element.

(a) First we have checked whether or not the queue is empty. The value of **front** in our case is 7, hence an element at the **front** position would get deleted.

(b) Next, we have checked if the value of **front** has become equal to **rear**. If it has, then the element we wish to remove is the only element of the queue. On removal of this element the queue would become empty and hence the values of **front** and **rear** are set to -1.

On deleting an element from the queue the value of **front** is set to 0 if it is equal to **MAX** - 1. Otherwise **front** is simply incremented by 1. Figure 6-6 shows the circular queue after deleting two elements from the queue that was earlier filled with 8 elements.

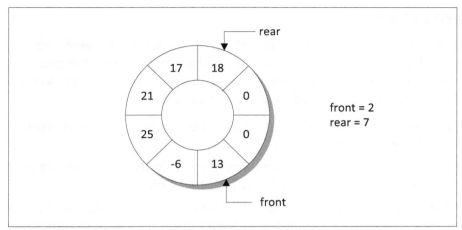

Figure 6-6. *Circular queue after deleting two elements.*

Deque

The word **deque** is a short form of double-ended queue and defines a data structure in which items can be added or deleted at either the front or rear end, but no changes can be made elsewhere in the list. Thus a deque is a generalization of both a stack and a queue. Figure 6-7 shows the representation of a deque.

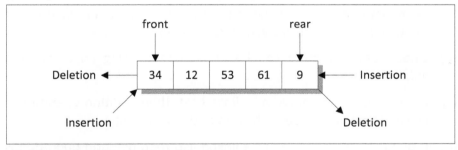

Figure 6-7. *Representation of a deque.*

There are two variations of a deque—an Input-restricted deque and an Output-restricted deque.

An Input restricted deque restricts the insertion of elements at one end only, but the deletion of elements can be done at both the ends of a queue.

On the contrary, an output-restricted deque, restricts the deletion of elements at one end only, and allows insertion to be done at both the ends of a deque.

Priority Queue

A priority queue is a collection of elements where the elements are stored according to their priority levels. The order in which the elements should get added or removed is decided by the priority of the element. Following rules are applied to maintain a priority queue.

(a) The element with a higher priority is processed before any element of lower priority.

(b) If there are elements with the same priority, then the element added first in the queue would get processed.

Priority queues are used for implementing job scheduling by the operating system where jobs with higher priorities are to be processed first. Another application of priority queues is simulation systems where priority corresponds to event times.

Chapter Bullets

Summary of chapter

(a) Queue data structure is a FIFO list in which addition of new elements takes place at the rear end of the queue and deletion of existing elements takes place at its front end.

(b) Queue data structure can be implemented using an array or a linked list.

(c) If queue is implemented as a linked list, then addition operation is like adding a new node at the end of the linked list.

(d) If queue is implemented as a linked list, then deletion operation is like deleting an existing node from the beginning of the linked list.

(e) There exist special types of queues like deque and priority queues.

Check Your Progress

Exercise - Level I

[A] Fill in the blanks:

(a) For a queue built using an array and containing **n** elements, the value of **front** would be _____ and **rear** would be _____.

(b) In a circular queue implemented using an array and holding 5 elements, if **front** is equal to **3** and **rear** is equal to **4**, then the new element would get placed at _____ position.

(c) A queue is called _____ when addition as well as deletion of elements can take place at both the ends.

(d) An _____ is a queue in which insertion of an element takes place at one end only but deletion occurs at both the ends.

(e) An _____ is a queue in which insertion of an element takes place at both the ends but deletion occurs at one end only.

Sharpen Your Skills

Exercise - Level II

[B] Choose the correct alternative for the following:

(a) Queue is a
   (1) Linear data structure
   (2) Non-linear data structure
   (3) Both (1) and (2)
   (4) None of the above

(b) The end at which a new element gets added to a queue is called
   (1) front
   (2) rear
   (3) top
   (4) bottom

(c) The end from which an element gets removed from the queue is called
   (1) front
   (2) rear
   (3) top
   (4) bottom

[C] Which of the following applications would be suitable for a queue.
   (1) A program is to keep track of patients as they check into a clinic, assigning them to doctors on a first-come, first-served basis.
   (2) An inventory of parts is to be processed by part number.
   (3) A dictionary of words used by spelling checker is to be created.

(4) Customers are to take numbers at a bakery and be served in order when their numbers come up.

Coding Interview Questions

Exercise Level III

[D] Write programs for the following:

(a) Write a program to represent a deque using a linked list. Also write functions to add and delete elements from the deque.

(b) Write a menu-driven program to simulate processing of batch jobs by a computer system. The scheduling of these jobs should be handled using a priority queue. The program should allow user to add or remove items from the queue. It should also display current status i.e. the total number of items in the queue.

(c) Write a program to copy one queue to another when the queue is implemented as a linked list.

Case Scenario Exercise

Priority Queues

Suppose there are several jobs to be performed with each job having a priority value of 1, 2, 3, 4, etc. Write a program that receives the job descriptions and the priorities. Create as many queues as the number of priorities and queue up the jobs into appropriate queues. For example, suppose the priorities are 1, 2, 3, and 4 and the data to be entered is as follows:

ABC, 2, XYZ, 1, PQR, 1, RTZ, 3, CBZ, 2, QQQ, 3, XXX, 4, RRR, 1

Then arrange these jobs as shown below:

Q1: XYZ, 1, PQR, 1, RRR, 1
Q2: ABC, 2, CBZ, 2

Q3: RTZ, 3, QQQ, 3

Q4: XXX, 4

The order of processing should be: Q1, Q2, Q3, Q4. Write a program to simulate the above problem.

07
Chapter

—

Trees
Of Herbs, Shrubs and Bushes

Why This Chapter Matters?

Nature is man's best teacher. In every walk of life
man has explored nature, learnt his lessons and
then applied the knowledge that nature offered him
to solve every-day problems that he faced at work-
place. It isn't without reason that there are data
structures like Trees, Binary Trees, Search Trees,
AVL Trees, Forests, etc. Trees are non-linear data
structures. They have many applications in
Computer Science, hence you must understand
them comprehensively.

If large input data is stored in a linked list then time required to access the data is prohibitive. In such cases a data structure called Tree is used. This data structure is often used in constructing the file systems and evaluation of arithmetic expressions. This data structure gives a running time of **O (log n)** for most operations.

Like linked lists, a tree also consists of several nodes. Each node may contain links that point to other nodes in the tree. So a tree can be used to represent a person and all of his descendants as shown in Figure 7-1.

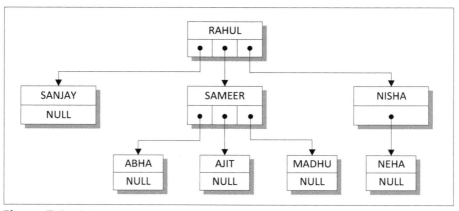

Figure 7-1. *A tree structure.*

Note that each node in this tree contains a name for data and one or more pointers to the other tree nodes. Although a tree may contain any number of pointers to the other tree nodes, a large number of have at the most two pointers to the other tree nodes. Such trees are called **Binary trees**.

Binary Trees

Let us begin our study of binary trees by discussing some basic concepts and terminology.

A binary tree is a finite set of elements that is either empty or is partitioned into three disjoint sub-sets. The first sub-set contains a single element called the **root** of the tree. The other two sub-sets are themselves binary trees, called the **left** and **right sub-trees** of the original tree. A left or right sub-tree can be empty.

Each element of a binary tree is called a **node** of the tree. The tree shown in Figure 7-2(a) consists of nine nodes with **A** as its root. Its left sub-tree is rooted at **B** and its right sub-tree is rooted at **C**. This is indicated by the two branches emanating from **A** to **B** on the left and to **C** on the right. The absence of a branch indicates an empty sub-tree. For example, the left sub-tree of the binary tree rooted at **C** and the right sub-tree of the binary tree rooted at **E** are both empty. The binary trees rooted at **D**, **G**, **H** and **I** have empty right and left sub-trees.

Figure 7-2(b) illustrates a structure that is not a binary tree.

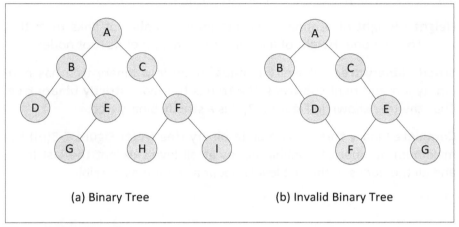

(a) Binary Tree   (b) Invalid Binary Tree

Figure 7-2. *Binary tree.*

Let us now learn some terminology used in association with binary trees.

Parent, Child : If **A** is the root of a binary tree and **B** is the root of its left or right sub-tree then, **A** is **parent** of **B** and **B** is **left** or **right child** of **A**.

Leaf : A node that has no children (such as **D**, **G**, **H**, or **I** in Figure 7-2(a)) is called a **leaf**.

Ancestor, Descendant : Any node **n1**, is an **ancestor** of node **n2** (and **n2** is a **descendant** of **n1**) if **n1** is either the parent of **n2** or the parent of some ancestor of **n2**. For example, in the tree shown in Figure 7-2(a), **A** is an ancestor of **C**.

Climbing, Descending : The root of the tree is at the top and the leaves at the bottom. Going from the leaves to the root is called **climbing** the tree, and going from the root to the leaves is called **descending** the tree.

Degree of a node : The number of nodes connected to a particular node is called the **degree** of a particular node. For example, in Figure 7-2(a) the node **B** has a degree 3. The degree of a leaf node is always one.

Level : The root of the tree has level 0. Level of any other node in the tree is one more than the level of its parent. For example, in the binary tree shown in Figure 7-2(a), node **E** is at level 2 and node **H** is at level 3.

Depth : **Depth** of a node is the maximum number of links from root to that node. The **depth** of a binary tree is the maximum level of any leaf in the tree. This equals the length of the longest path from the root to any leaf. Thus the depth of the tree shown in Figure 7-2(a) is 3.

Height : **Height** of a node is the maximum number of links from that node to leaf node. **Height** of a binary tree is height of its root node.

Strictly binary tree : If every non-leaf node in a binary tree has non-empty left and right sub-trees, the tree is termed a **strictly binary tree**. Thus the tree shown in Figure 7-3(a) is a strictly binary tree.

Complete binary tree : A complete binary tree (refer Figure 7-3(b)) has maximum number of possible nodes at all levels except the last level, and all the nodes of the last level appear as far left as possible.

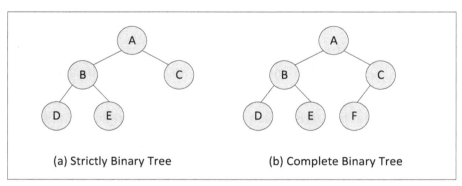

(a) Strictly Binary Tree   (b) Complete Binary Tree

Figure 7-3. *Strictly and Complete binary tree.*

Representation of Binary Trees in Memory

There are two ways by which we can represent a binary tree—Linked representation and Array representation. Both these ways are discussed below.

Linked Representation of Binary Trees

In liked representation each node contains addresses of its left child and right child. If a child is absent, the link contains a NULL value. For example, in Figure 7-4 the link fields of node **C** contain the address of the nodes **F** and **G**. The left link field of node **E** contains the address of the node **H**. Similarly, the right link contains a **NULL** as E has no right child. The nodes **D**, **F**, **G** and **H** contain a **NULL** value in both their link fields, as these are the leaf nodes.

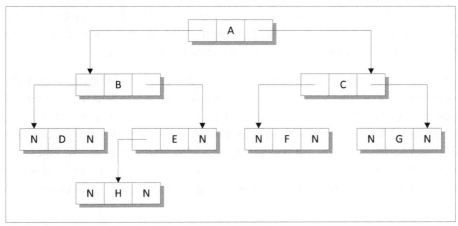

Figure 7-4. *Linked representation of a Binary tree.*

Array Representation of Binary Trees

When a binary tree is represented by arrays three separate arrays are required. One array **arr** stores the data fields of the trees. The other two arrays **lc** and **rc** represents the left child and right child of the nodes. Figure 7-5 shows these three arrays, which represents the tree shown in Figure 7-4.

arr	A	B	C	D	E	F	G	'\0'	'\0'	H
lc	1	3	5	-1	9	-1	-1	-1	-1	-1
rc	2	4	6	-1	-1	-1	-1	-1	-1	-1

Figure 7-5. *Array representation of a binary tree.*

The array **lc** and **rc** contains the index of the array **arr** where the data is present. If the node does not have any left child or right child then the element of the array **lc** or **rc** contains a value -1. The 0th element of the array **arr** contains the root node data. Some elements of the array **arr** contain '\0' which represents an empty child.

Suppose we wish to find the left and right child of the node **E.** Then we need to find the value present at index 4 in array **lc** and **rc** since **E** is present at index 4 in the array **arr.** The value present at index 4 in the array **lc** is 9, which is the index position of node **H** in the array **arr.** So the left child of the node **E** is **H.** The right child of the node **E** is empty because the value present at index 4 in the array **rc** is −1.

We can also represent a binary tree using one single array. For this, numbers are given to each node starting from the root node— 0 to root node, 1 to the left node of the first level, then 2 to the second node from left of the first level and so on. In other words, the nodes are numbered from left to right level by level from top to bottom. Figure 7-6(a) shows the numbers given to each node in the tree. Note that while numbering the nodes of the tree, empty nodes are also taken into account.

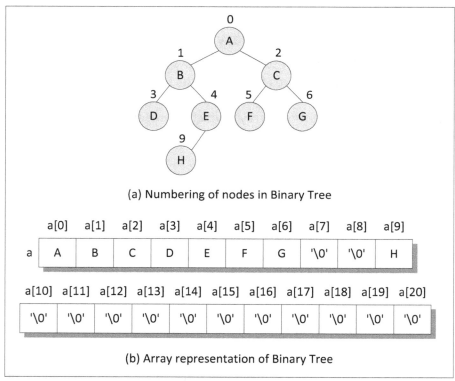

(a) Numbering of nodes in Binary Tree

a[0]	a[1]	a[2]	a[3]	a[4]	a[5]	a[6]	a[7]	a[8]	a[9]
A	B	C	D	E	F	G	'\0'	'\0'	H

a (label at left)

a[10]	a[11]	a[12]	a[13]	a[14]	a[15]	a[16]	a[17]	a[18]	a[19]	a[20]
'\0'	'\0'	'\0'	'\0'	'\0'	'\0'	'\0'	'\0'	'\0'	'\0'	'\0'

(b) Array representation of Binary Tree

Figure 7-6. *Array representation of binary tree using one array.*

It can be observed that if **n** is the number given to the node then its left child is at position **(2n + 1)** in the array and right child at position **(2n +**

2). If any node doesn't have a left or a right child then an empty node is assumed and a value '\0' is stored at that index in the array.

Binary Search Trees

Binary search tree (BST) is a variant of binary tree in which the nodes are arranged in a particular manner. A BST has the property that all the elements in the left sub-tree of a node **n** are less than **n** and all the elements in the right sub-tree of **n** are greater than or equal to **n**. Figure 7-7 shows a few BSTs.

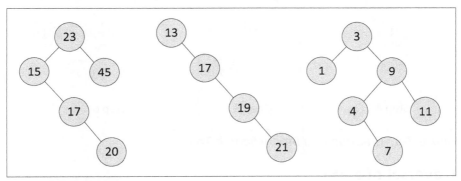

Figure 7-7. *Sample BSTs.*

Operations on a Binary Search Tree

There are many operations that can be performed on binary search trees. Insertion, Traversal, Searching and Deletion are the most basic amongst them. Let us now discuss these operations in detail.

Insertion of a Node

While inserting a node in a BST the value being inserted is compared with the root node. A left sub-tree is taken if the value is smaller than the root node and a right sub-tree if it is greater or equal to the node. This operation is repeated at each level till a node is found whose left or right sub-tree is empty. Finally, the new node is appropriately made the left or right child of this node.

If the input list is 3, 9, 1, 4, 7, 11, then Figure 7-8 shows the stepwise insertion of new nodes in a BST.

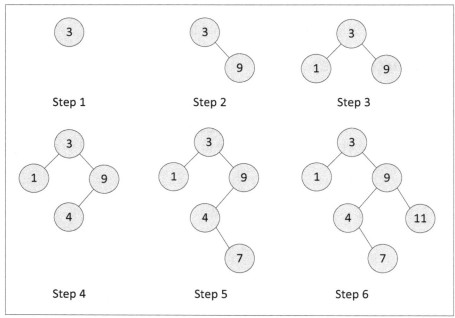

Figure 7-8. *Creation of a Binary Search Tree.*

Traversal of a BST

The traversal of a BST is to visit each node in the tree exactly once. There are three popular methods of BST traversal—**in-order** traversal, **pre-order** traversal and **post-order** traversal. In each of these methods nothing needs be done to traverse an empty BST.

Recall that each sub-tree of a BST is a BST itself. Thus, traversing a BST involves visiting the root node and traversing its left and right sub-trees. The only difference among the methods is the order in which these three operations are performed.

To traverse a non-empty BST in pre-order, we perform the following three operations:

(1) Visit the root
(2) Traverse the left sub-tree in pre-order
(3) Traverse the right sub-tree in pre-order

To traverse a non-empty BST in in-order (or symmetric order):

(1) Traverse the left sub-tree in in-order
(2) Visit the root
(3) Traverse the right sub-tree in in-order

To traverse a non-empty BST in post-order:

(4) Travesrse the left sub-tree in post-order
(5) Traverse the right sub-tree in post-order
(6) Visit the root

Figure 7-9 shows the order of visiting nodes using these traversal methods for the given BST.

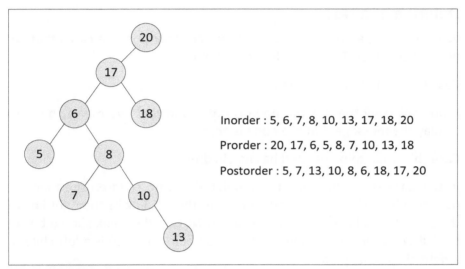

Inorder : 5, 6, 7, 8, 10, 13, 17, 18, 20

Prorder : 20, 17, 6, 5, 8, 7, 10, 13, 18

Postorder : 5, 7, 13, 10, 8, 6, 18, 17, 20

Figure 7-9. *Traversals of binary tree.*

Searching of a Node

To search any node in a binary tree, initially the value to be searched is compared with the root node. If they match then the search is successful. If the value is greater than the root node then searching process proceeds in the right sub-tree of the root node, otherwise, it proceeds in the left sub-tree of the root node.

BST search operation is very efficient because while searching an element we do not need to traverse the entire tree. At every node, we get a hint regarding which sub-tree to search in. For example, in the BST shown in Figure 7-8 step 6, if we have to search for 7, then we know that we have to scan only the right sub-tree since 7 is greater than 3. Likewise, when we descend down the tree and reach 9 we have to search only its left sub-tree as 7 is less than 9.

Since at every step we eliminate half of the sub-tree from the search process the average search time is $O(\log_2 n)$. Same applies to insertion or deletion of an element in a BST. As against this, in a sorted array, even though searching can be done in $O(\log_2 n)$ time, insertion and deletion times are high. In contrast, insertion and deletion of elements in a linked list is easier, but searching takes O(n) time.

Due to this efficiency BSTs are widely used in dictionary problems where insertion, deletion and search are done on the basis of some indexed key value.

Deletion of a Node

While deleting a node from a BST there are four possible cases that we need to consider. These are discussed below.

Case (a): Node to be deleted is absent.

If on traversing the BST the node is not found then we merely need to display the message that the node is absent.

Case (b): Node to be deleted has no children

In this case since the node to be deleted has no children the memory occupied by it should be freed and either the left link or the right link of the parent of this node should be set to **NULL**. Which link should be set to **NULL** depends upon whether the node being deleted is a left child or a right child of its parent.

Case (c): Node to be deleted has one child

In this case we have to adjust the pointer of the parent of the node to be deleted such that after deletion it points to the child of the node being deleted. This is shown in Figure 7-10.

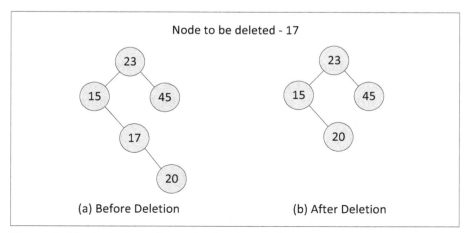

Figure 7-10. *Deletion of a node that has only one child.*

Case (d): Node to be deleted has two children

This is a more complex case. Consider node 23 shown in Figure 7-11(a). The in-order successor of the node 23 is node 45. The in-order successor should now be copied into the node to be deleted and a pointer should be set up pointing to the in-order successor (node 45). The in-order successor would always have one or zero child. This in-order successor should then be deleted using the same procedure as for deleting a one child or a zero child node.

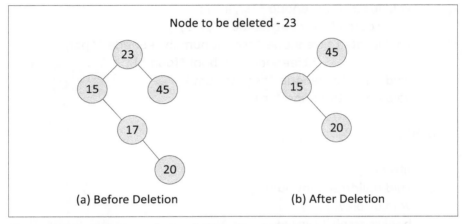

Node to be deleted - 23

(a) Before Deletion   (b) After Deletion

Figure 7-11. *Deletion of a node that has both left and right child.*

A program that implements the different operations on a BST is given below:

Honest Solid Code   {C++}

Program 7-1. Implementation of various BST operations

```cpp
#include <iostream>
using namespace std ;

struct btreenode
{
    btreenode *leftchild ;
    int data ;
    btreenode *rightchild ;
} ;
```

```
class btree
{
    private :

        btreenode *root ;

        void inorder ( btreenode *sr ) ;
        void preorder ( btreenode *sr ) ;
        void postorder ( btreenode *sr ) ;
        void insert ( btreenode **sr, int ) ;
        bool search ( struct btreenode *, int ) ;
        void locate ( btreenode **sr, int num, btreenode **par,
                        btreenode **x, bool *found ) ;
        void rem ( btreenode **sr, int num ) ;
        void del ( btreenode *sr ) ;

    public :

        btree( ) ;
        void buildtree ( int num ) ;
        void display( ) ;
        bool searchbst ( int ) ;
        void remove ( int num ) ;
        ~btree( ) ;
} ;

// initialises data members
btree :: btree( )
{
    root = NULL ;
}

// calls insert( ) to build tree
void btree :: buildtree ( int num )
{
    insert ( &root, num ) ;
}

// inserts a new node in a binary search tree
void btree :: insert ( btreenode **sr, int num )
{
```

```cpp
    if ( *sr == NULL )
    {
        *sr = new btreenode ;
        ( *sr )->leftchild = NULL ;
        ( *sr )->data = num ;
        ( *sr )->rightchild = NULL ;
    }
    else  // search the node to which new node will be attached
    {
        // if new data is less, traverse to left
        if ( num < ( *sr )->data )
            insert ( & ( ( *sr )->leftchild ), num ) ;
        else
            // else traverse to right
            insert ( & ( ( *sr )->rightchild ), num ) ;
    }
}

// calls inorder( ) to traverse tree
void btree :: display( )
{
    cout << endl << "Inorder: " ;
    inorder ( root ) ;
    cout << endl << "Preorder: " ;
    preorder ( root ) ;
    cout << endl << "Postorder: " ;
    postorder ( root ) ;

}

// traverse BST in Left-Root-Right fashion
void btree :: inorder ( btreenode *sr )
{
    if ( sr != NULL )
    {
        inorder ( sr->leftchild ) ;
        cout << sr->data << "\t" ;
        inorder ( sr->rightchild ) ;
    }
}
```

```
// traverse BST in Root-Left-Right fashion
void btree :: preorder ( btreenode *sr )
{
    if ( sr != NULL )
    {
        cout << sr->data << "\t" ;
        preorder ( sr->leftchild ) ;
        preorder ( sr->rightchild ) ;
    }
}

// traverse BST in Left-Right-Root fashion
void btree :: postorder ( btreenode *sr )
{
    if ( sr != NULL )
    {
        postorder ( sr->leftchild ) ;
        postorder ( sr->rightchild ) ;
        cout << sr->data << "\t" ;
    }
}

bool btree :: searchbst ( int num )
{
    bool flag ;
    flag = search ( root, num ) ;
    return flag ;
}

/* search BST */
bool btree :: search ( struct btreenode *sr, int num )
{
    while ( sr != NULL )
    {
        if ( num == sr->data )
            return true ;
        else if ( num < sr->data )
            sr = sr->leftchild ;
        else
            sr = sr->rightchild ;
    }
```

```
        return false ;
}

// calls rem to delete node
void btree :: remove ( int num )
{
    rem ( &root, num ) ;
}

// deletes a node from the BST
void btree :: rem ( btreenode **sr, int num )
{
    bool found ;
    btreenode *parent, *x, *xsucc ;

    // if tree is empty
    if ( *sr == NULL )
    {
        cout << endl << "Tree is empty" ;
        return ;
    }

    parent = x = NULL ;

    // call to search function to find the node to be deleted
    locate ( sr, num, &parent, &x, &found ) ;

    // if the node to deleted is not found
    if ( found == false )
    {
        cout << endl << "Data to be deleted, not found" ;
        return ;
    }

    // if the node to be deleted has two children
    if ( x->leftchild != NULL && x->rightchild != NULL )
    {
        parent = x ;
        xsucc = x->rightchild ;

        while ( xsucc->leftchild != NULL )
```

```
        {
            parent = xsucc ;
            xsucc = xsucc->leftchild ;
        }

        x->data = xsucc->data ;
        x = xsucc ;
    }

    // if the node to be deleted has no child
    if ( x->leftchild == NULL && x->rightchild == NULL )
    {
        if ( parent->rightchild == x )
            parent->rightchild = NULL ;
        else
            parent->leftchild = NULL ;

        delete x ;
        return ;
    }

    // if the node to be deleted has only rightchild
    if ( x->leftchild == NULL && x->rightchild != NULL )
    {
        if ( parent->leftchild == x )
            parent->leftchild = x->rightchild ;
        else
            parent->rightchild = x->rightchild ;

        delete x ;
        return ;
    }

    // if the node to be deleted has only left child
    if ( x->leftchild != NULL && x->rightchild == NULL )
    {
        if ( parent->leftchild == x )
            parent->leftchild = x->leftchild ;
        else
            parent->rightchild = x->leftchild ;
```

```
            delete x ;
            return ;
        }
    }
}

// returns the address of the node to be deleted, address of its parent
// and whether the node is found or not
void btree :: locate ( btreenode **sr, int num, btreenode **par,
                        btreenode **x, bool *found )
{
    btreenode *q ;

    q = *sr ;
    *found = false ;
    *par = NULL ;

    while ( q != NULL )
    {
        // if the node to be deleted is found
        if ( q->data == num )
        {
            *found = true ;
            *x = q ;
            return ;
        }

        *par = q ;

        if ( q->data > num )
            q = q->leftchild ;
        else
            q = q->rightchild ;
    }
}

// calls del to deallocate memory
btree :: ~btree( )
{
    del ( root ) ;
}
```

```
// deletes nodes of a BST
void btree :: del ( btreenode *sr )
{
    if ( sr != NULL )
    {
        del ( sr->leftchild ) ;
        del ( sr->rightchild ) ;
    }
    delete sr ;
}

int main( )
{
    btree bt ;
    int i, a[ ] = { 20, 17, 6, 18, 8, 5, 7, 10, 13  } ;
    bool flag ;

    for ( i = 0 ; i <= 8 ; i++ )
        bt.buildtree ( a[i] ) ;

    cout << endl << "BST after insertion:" ;
    bt.display( ) ;

    flag = bt.searchbst ( 13 ) ;
    if ( flag == true )
        cout << endl << "Node 13 found in BST" ;
    else
        cout << endl << "Node 13 not found in BST" ;

    bt.remove ( 10 ) ;
    cout << endl << "BST after deleting 10:" ;
    bt.display( ) ;

    bt.remove ( 14 ) ;
    cout << endl << "BST after deleting 14:" ;
    bt.display( ) ;

    bt.remove ( 8 ) ;
    cout << endl << "BST after deleting 8:" ;
    bt.display( ) ;
```

```
    return 0 ;
}
```

Output:

```
BST after insertion:
Inorder: 5    6    7    8    10    13    17    18    20
Preorder: 20   17   6    5    8     7     10    13    18
Postorder: 5   7    13   10   8     6     18    17    20
Node 13 found in BST
BST after deleting 10:
Inorder: 5    6    7    8    13    17    18    20
Preorder: 20   17   6    5    8     7     13    18
Postorder: 5   7    13   8    6     18    17    20
Node to be deleted not found
BST after deleting 14:
Inorder: 5    6    7    8    13    17    18    20
Preorder: 20   17   6    5    8     7     13    18
Postorder: 5   7    13   8    6     18    17    20
BST after deleting 8:
Inorder: 5    6    7    13    17    18    20
Preorder: 20   17   6    5    13    7     18
Postorder: 5   7    13   6    18    17    20
```

In **main( )**, when the object **bt** of type **btree** is created the constructor sets the pointer to the root node of BST to NULL indicating the BST is empty to begin with. Then the **buildtree( )** function is called repeatedly to insert nodes in the BST. This function in turn calls the **insert( )** function. Two arguments are passed to **insert( )**—address of pointer to the root node of BST and data that is to be inserted.

In the **insert( )** function it is ascertained whether BST is empty or not. If it is empty then a new node is created and the data to be inserted is stored in it. The left and right child of this new node is set with a **NULL** value, as this is the first node being inserted.

If BST is not empty then the current node is compared with the data to be inserted and **insert( )** function is called recursively to insert the node in the left/right sub-tree. Thus **insert( )** continues to move down the levels of BST until it reaches a leaf node. When it does, the new node gets inserted in the left/right sub-tree.

Once all nodes are inserted, the **display( )** function is called to display all the nodes present in the BST. This function in turn calls **inorder( )**, **preorder( )** and **postorder( )**.

 inorder( ) is called to traverse BST as per in-order traversal. This function receives address of the root node. A condition is checked whether the pointer is **NULL**. If the pointer is not **NULL** then a recursive call is made first for traversing the left sub-tree and then for traversing the right sub-tree. In between these two recursive calls, the data of the current node is printed.

The functions **preorder( )** and **postorder( )** work in the same manner except for a small difference. In case of the function **preorder( )** initially node's data is printed then the recursive calls are made for the left and right sub-trees. On the other hand, in case of **postorder( )** firstly the recursive calls for left and right sub-trees are made and then the node's data is printed.

The function **searchbst( )** searches for the given data in the BST by calling **search( )**. The searching is done in a **while** loop. If the node is found then true is returned. If not, then we either go to the left or right sub-tree depending upon whether the node being searched has a value less than or greater than the current node's data. If control goes beyond the **while** loop it means that node being searched is not present in the BST. In this case false is returned.

The **remove( )** function is used to delete a node in BST. It calls the **rem( )** function. This function calls **locate( )** to search the node to be deleted. If the node is found, **locate( )** sets up the address of the node to be deleted in **x**, address of its parent in **parent** and true/false in **found** depending upon whether the node is found or not. If node to be deleted is not found then an appropriate message is displayed.

If the node to be deleted is found then one of the following four cases would arise:

(a) the node has two children

(b) the node has no child

(c) the node has only right child

(d) the node has only left child

How each of these cases is tackled has already been discussed in the previous section.

When **main( )** ends, the destructor of **btree** class gets called. It calls the **del( )** function to delete all the nodes present in BST. Note that functions **inorder( )**, **preorder( )**, **postorder( )**, **insert( )**, **search( )**, **locate( )**, **rem( )** and **del( )** have been declared as **private** functions in the **btree** class as they are not accessed directly from **main( )**.

Reconstruction of a Binary Tree

If we know the sequence of nodes obtained through in-order/pre-order/post-order traversal it may not be feasible to reconstruct the binary tree. This is because two different binary trees may yield same sequence of nodes when traversed using post-order traversal. Similarly, in-order or pre-order traversal of different binary trees may yield the same sequence of nodes. However, we can construct a unique binary tree if the results of in-order and pre-order traversal are available. Let us understand this with the help of following set of in-order and pre-order traversal results:

In-order traversal: 4, 7, 2, 8, 5, 1, 6, 9, 3
Pre-order traversal: 1, 2, 4, 7, 5, 8, 3, 6, 9

We know that the first value in the pre-order traversal gives us the root of the binary tree. So the node with data 1 becomes the root of the binary tree. In in-order traversal, initially the left sub-tree is traversed then the root node and then the right sub-tree. So the data before 1 in the in-order list (i.e. 4, 7, 2, 8, 5) forms the left sub-tree and the data after 1 in the in-order list (i.e. 6, 9, 3) forms the right sub-tree. In Figure 7-12(a) the structure of tree is shown after separating the tree in left and right sub-trees.

Now look at the left sub-tree. The data in pre-order list is 2, so the root node of the left sub-tree is 2. Hence data before 2 in the in-order list (i.e. 4, 7) will form the left sub-tree of the node that contains a value 2. The data that comes to the right of 2 in the in-order list (i.e. 8, 5) forms the right sub-tree of the node with value 2. Figure 7-12(b) shows structure of tree after expanding the left and right sub-tree of the node that contains a value 2.

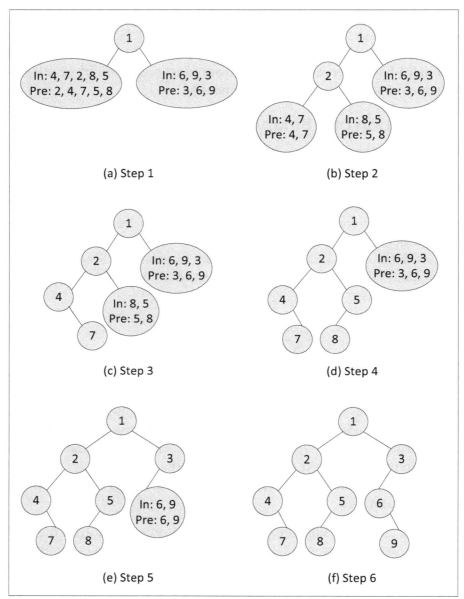

Figure 7-12. *Reconstruction of a binary tree.*

Now the next data in pre-order list is 4, so the root node of the left sub-tree of the node that contains a value 2 is 4. The data before 4 in the in-order list forms the left sub-tree of the node that contains a value 4. But as there is no data present before 4 in in-order list, the left sub-tree of the node with value 4 is empty. The data that comes to the right of 4 in the in-order list (i.e. 7) forms the right sub-tree of the node that contains a value 4. Figure 7-12(c) shows structure of tree after expanding the left and right sub-tree of the node that contains a value 4.

In the same way one by one all the data are picked from the pre-order list and are placed and their respective sub-trees are constructed. Figure 7-12(d) to 7-12(f) shows each step of this construction process.

Threaded Binary Tree

In the linked representation of a binary tree, many nodes contain a NULL pointer, either in their left or right fields or in both. Instead of wasting space in storing a NULL pointer, it can be efficiently used to store pointer to the in-order predecessor or the in-order successor of the node. These special pointers are called threads and binary trees containing threads are called **threaded binary trees**.

In threaded binary trees the pointers that point to in-order successor of a node are called **right threads**. Likewise, pointers that point to in-order predecessor of a node are called **left threads**. The threads are typically denoted using arrows as shown in Figure 7-13.

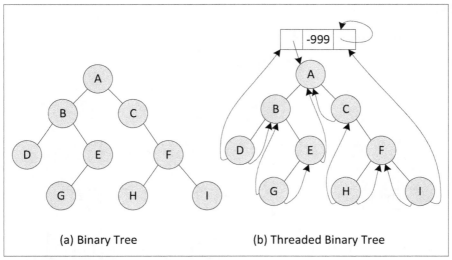

(a) Binary Tree   (b) Threaded Binary Tree

Figure 7-13. *Threaded binary tree.*

Figure 7-13(b) shows a head node containing a value -999. The entire binary tree is shown as the left child of this head node. The right link of the head node points to itself. This head node is useful while creating programs for threaded binary tree. For example, while traversing the tree we can start with head node, visit each node and stop the traversal when we reach the head node once again. Note that in Figure 7-13(b) predecessor of node D and successor of node I point to the head node as they happen to be first and last node in the in-order traversal sequence.

In a program to help us distinguish between a pointer and a thread, the structure that represents a node contains two additional fields, **leftflag** and **rightflag**. If they contain a true they represent a thread, and if they contain a false, then they represent a pointer to a child node. The structure declaration for a node would be as shown below.

```
struct thtree
{
    enum boolean leftflag ;
    struct thtree *left ;
    int data ;
    struct thtree *right ;
    enum boolean rightflag ;
} ;
```

A threaded binary tree created using this structure is shown in Figure 7-14.

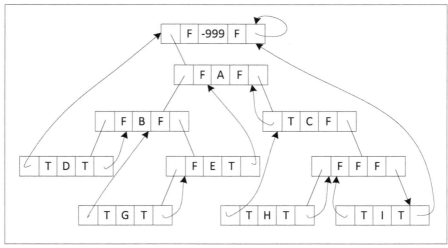

Figure 7-14. *Threaded binary tree showing links and threads.*

Let us now write a program that inserts nodes in a threaded binary tree and visits each node in in-order traversal.

Honest Solid Code

{C++}

Program 7-2. Implementation of threaded binary tree

```cpp
#include <iostream>
using namespace std ;

class ttree
{
    private :

        struct thtree
        {
            bool left ;
            thtree *leftchild ;
            int data ;
            thtree *rightchild ;
            bool right ;
        } *th_head ;

    public :

        ttree( ) ;
        void insert ( int num ) ;
        void inorder( ) ;
} ;

// initialises data member
ttree :: ttree( )
{
    th_head = NULL ;
}

// inserts a node in a threaded binary tree
void ttree :: insert ( int num )
{
    thtree *head = th_head, *p, *z ;

    // allocating a new node
    z = new thtree ;
```

```
    z->left = true ;  // indicates a thread
    z->data = num ;   // assign new data
    z->right = true ;  // indicates a thread

    // if tree is empty
    if ( th_head == NULL )
    {
        head = new thtree ;

        // entire tree is treated as left sub-tree of head node
        head->left = false ;

        head->leftchild = z ;  // z becomes leftchild of the head node
        head->data = -9999 ;  // no data
        head->rightchild = head ; // right link points to head node
        head->right = false ;

        th_head = head ;
        z->leftchild = head ;
        z->rightchild = head ;
    }
    else  // if tree is non-empty
    {
        p = head->leftchild ;

        // traverse till we reach head
        while ( p != head )
        {
            if ( p->data > num )
            {
                // check for a thread
                if ( p->left != true )
                    p = p->leftchild ;
                else
                {
                    z->leftchild = p->leftchild ;
                    p->leftchild = z ;
                    p->left = false ;
                    z->right = true ;
                    z->rightchild = p ;
                    return ;
```

```
                    }
                }
                else
                {
                    if ( p->data < num )
                    {
                        if ( p->right != true )
                            p = p->rightchild ;
                        else
                        {
                            z->rightchild = p->rightchild ;
                            p->rightchild = z ;
                            p->right = false ;
                            z->left = true ;
                            z->leftchild = p ;
                            return ;
                        }
                    }
                }
            }
        }
    }
}


// traverses the threaded binary tree in in-order
void ttree :: inorder( )
{
    thtree *p ;

    p = th_head->leftchild ;

    while ( p != th_head )
    {
        while ( p->left == false )
            p = p->leftchild ;

        cout << p->data <<  "\t" ;

        while ( p->right == true )
        {
            p = p->rightchild ;
```

```
        if ( p == th_head )
            break ;

        cout << p->data << "\t" ;

    }
    p = p->rightchild ;
  }
}

int main( )
{
    ttree th ;

    th.insert ( 11 ) ;  th.insert ( 9 ) ;
    th.insert ( 13 ) ;  th.insert ( 8 ) ;
    th.insert ( 10 ) ;  th.insert ( 12 ) ;
    th.insert ( 14 ) ;  th.insert ( 15 ) ;
    th.insert ( 7 ) ;

    cout << "Threaded binary tree:" << endl ;
    th.inorder( ) ;

    return 0 ;
}
```

Output:

```
Threaded binary tree:
7    8    9    10    11    12    13    14    15
```

Now, a brief explanation about the program. For each node we have used **bool** variables **left/right** to store information whether the pointer **leftchild/rightchild** is a thread or a link.

To insert a new node in the threaded BST, the **insert( )** function is called. It first checks for an empty tree. If the tree is empty then firstly a head node is created. Then the node being inserted is made its left sub-tree with both links set up as threads. Otherwise, the node is inserted at an appropriate place by traversing the tree such that the BST nature of the tree is preserved.

The threaded binary tree's in-order traversal is different than a normal tree in the sense that we do not have to stack the pointers to nodes visited earlier so as to reach them later. This is avoided by using the threads to ancestors. The procedure to achieve this is as follows:

This procedure begins by first going to the left sub-tree of the head node. Then through a **while** loop we follow the left pointers until a thread to a predecessor is found. On encountering this thread, we print the data for the leftmost node. Next, through another **while** loop we follow the thread back up to the ancestor node and print this ancestor node's data. This way we continue to move up till **right** is a thread. When we reach a link we go to the right child and again follow the same procedure by checking its left sub-tree.

As we follow these steps we are sometimes likely to reach the head node, and that is the time to stop the procedure.

AVL Trees

We know that height of a BST is the maximum number of edges from leaf node to root node. Note that if we change the order of insertion of nodes in a BST, we may get BSTs of different heights. As a confirmation, you may try creating two BSTs using the insertion order as 30, 40, 10, 50, 20, 5, 35 and 50, 40, 35, 30, 20, 10, 5. In the first case you would get a BST of height 2 and in the second case a BST of height 6.

Also, search time in a BST depends upon its height. Searching is efficient if the heights of both left and right sub-trees of any node are equal. However, frequent insertions and deletions in a BST are likely to make it unbalanced. The efficiency of searching is ideal if the difference between the heights of left and right sub-trees of all the nodes in a BST is at the most one. Such a binary search tree is called a **Balanced BST**. It was invented in the year 1962 by two Russian mathematicians—G. M. Adelson-Velskii and E. M. Landis. Hence such trees are also known as AVL trees. Figure 7-15 shows some examples of AVL trees.

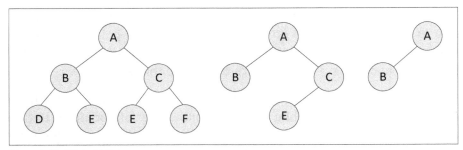

Figure 7-15. *AVL trees.*

The balance factor of a node is calculated as height of the left sub-tree minus height of the right sub-tree of the node. The balance factor of any node in an AVL BST should be -1, 0 or 1. If it is other than these three values then the tree is not balanced.

To re-balance and make it an AVL tree the nodes need to be properly adjusted. This is done by doing one of the 4 types of rotations—Left rotation, Right rotation, Left Right rotation and Right Left rotation. Of these, first two involve a 1 step process, whereas the next two involve a 2 step process.

Figure 7-16 shows LL, RR, LR and RL imbalances and how to correct them by doing appropriate rotations.

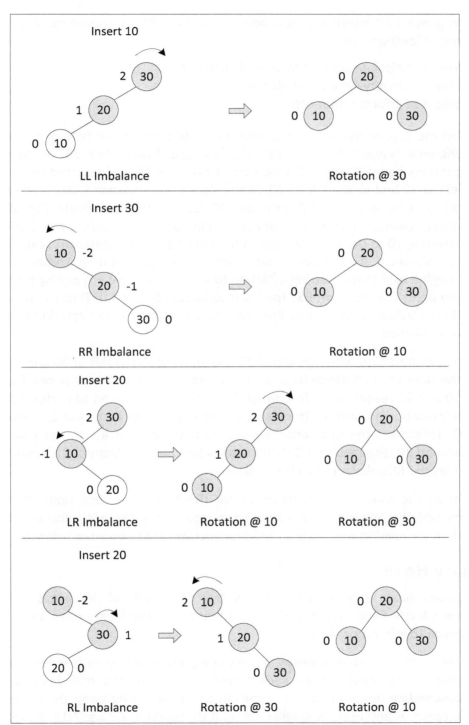

Figure 7-16. *LL, RR, LR and RL imbalances and rotations.*

In general on inserting a new node in an AVL BST we should carry out the following steps:

Step 1 : Calculate balance factors of all nodes
Step 2 : Identify type of imbalance
Step 3 : Perform rotation(s)

Let me explain the imbalances and the rotations with the help of cases shown in Figure 7-16. Let us take the first case. Assume that BST already contains nodes 30 and 20. When we insert node 10, it is inserted to the left of 30 and to the left of 20. Now calculate the balance factors. They turn out to be 2, 1 and 0 for nodes 30, 20 and 10 respectively. Out of these, balance factor 2 is unacceptable. Since this was caused by inserting 10 to the left of 30 and to the left of 20, this imbalance is called LL imbalance. To correct it, we need to do right rotation about 30. Imagine as if there is string attached to node 30 and we are pulling it to the right. The resultant BST has balance factors 0, 0 and 0. Thus the tree is now balanced. On similar lines RR imbalance and the left rotation can be explained.

In the third case when we insert 20 it is inserted to the left of 30 and to the right of 20. Balance factors turn out to be 2, -1 and 0 for nodes 30, 10 and 20 respectively. To correct the imbalance we need to perform a left rotation around 10. The resultant BST has balance factors of 2, 1 and 0. To correct the imbalance we should now perform a right rotation around 30. The resultant BST has satisfactory balance factors. On similar lines the RL imbalance can be explained.

In all the four cases discussed above there was only one node that caused the imbalance. In some other case if 2 nodes are unbalanced then we need to rotate about the first ancestor that caused imbalance.

Binary Heap

Binary heap is a complete binary tree. It means all its levels are completely filled except perhaps last and at the last level nodes are as much to left as possible.

There are two types of heaps. If the value present at any node is greater than all its children then such a tree is called as the **max heap** or **descending heap**. In case of a **min heap** or **ascending heap** the value present in any node is smaller than all its children. Figure 7-17 shows these two types of heaps.

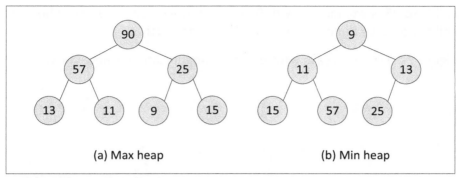

Figure 7-17. *Types of heaps.*

One of the common operations carried out while using a binary heap is heapification of a node. While heapifying a node in a max heap, we need to ensure that all its children satisfy the heap property—Parent >= Left child, Right child. This operation involves following steps:

(a) Pick maximum out of given node, and its left and right child

(b) If maximum is root, do nothing

(c) If maximum is left, exchange root with left and heapify left node

(d) If maximum is right, exchange root with right and heapify right node

These operations are shown in Figure 7-18.

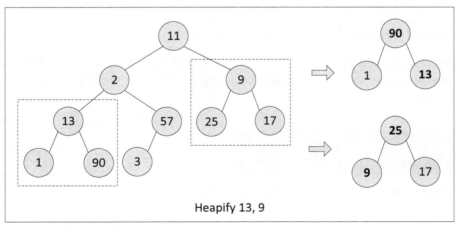

Heapify 13, 9

Figure 7-18. *Heapify operation.*

Note that in the binary tree shown in Figure 7-18 node 13 and node 9 were violating the heap property. While heapifying 13, maximum out of 13, 1, and 90 is 90. Since 90 is the right child it is exchanged with 13. As against this, while heapifying 9, maximum (25) turns out to be the left child. So 25 is exchanged with 9. Since after exchange 13 and 9 became child nodes, we did not have to heapify them further.

Figure 7-19 shows a case where further heapification is necessary.

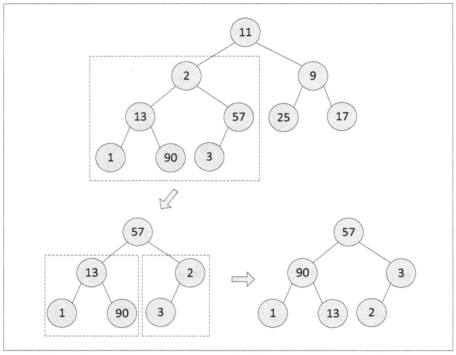

Figure 7-19. *Multi-step heapify operation.*

Let us now see how see how we can create max heap out of a binary tree programmatically. We will be using an array to store the nodes in the binary tree.

Honest Solid Code   {C++}

Program 7-3. Construction of max heap

```cpp
#include <iostream>
using namespace std ;

void heapify ( int [ ], int, int ) ;

int main( )
```

```
{
    int  arr[ ] = { 11, 2, 9, 13, 3, 25, 17, 1, 90, 57 } ;
    int  i, size ;

    size = 10 ;
    for ( i = size / 2 - 1 ; i >= 0 ; i-- )
        heapify ( arr, size, i ) ;

    for ( i = 0 ; i < size ; i ++ )
        cout << arr[ i ] << "\t" ;
}

void heapify ( int arr[ ], int sz, int i )
{
    int largest, lch, rch, t ;

    lch = 2 * i + 1 ;
    rch = 2 * i + 2 ;

    if ( lch >= sz )
        return ;

    largest = i ;
    /* if left child is larger than root */
    if ( lch < sz && arr[ lch ] > arr[ largest ] )
        largest = lch ;

    /* if right child is larger than largest so far */
    if ( rch < sz && arr[ rch ] > arr[ largest ] )
        largest = rch ;

    /* if largest is not root */
    if ( largest != i )
    {
        t = arr[ i ] ;
        arr[ i ] = arr[ largest ] ;
        arr[ largest ] = t ;

        /* heapify the affected sub-tree */
        heapify ( arr, sz, largest ) ;
    }
```

}

Output:

90   57   25   13   11   9   17   1   2   3

On execution of the program the binary tress shown in Figure 7-20(a) gets converted into a max heap shown in Figure 7-20(b).

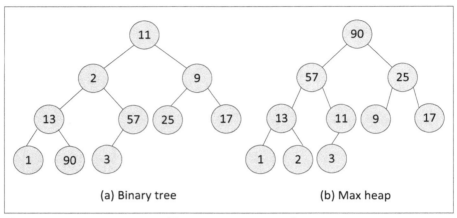

Figure 7-20. *Conversion of binary tree to max heap.*

The program begins by declaring an array that represents the binary tree. We know that in array representation of a binary tree, a node at location **i** has its left and right child at locations **(2i + 1)** and **(2i + 2)** respectively. Next, in the **for** loop we have repeatedly called **heapify( )** moving level by level from leaf towards root, and at any level from right to left, starting from node at location **size / 2 -1**. The **heapify( )** function finds the largest out of given node, and its left and right child.

If the given node turns out to be largest then it does nothing. But if left/right child turns out to be largest it exchanges the given node with left/right child and then proceeds to heapify the left/right child.

Binary heap is used in many areas of computer science. Some of these are listed below.

(a)   Finding minimum spanning tree

(b)   Finding the shortest path in a network of cities

(c)   Implementing priority queues

(d)   Merging K sorted arrays

Chapter Bullets

Summary of chapter

(a) Tree is a non-linear data structure.

(b) Each node in a binary tree can have 0, 1 or 2 children.

(c) Unlike trees in nature a binary tree has root at the top and leaves at the bottom with root node at level 0.

(d) Depth of a node is largest number of links from root to that node.

(e) Height of a node is largest number of links from leaf node to that node.

(f) A binary tree can be traversed in in-order, pre-order and post-order fashion

(g) If we know any two sequences out of in-order, pre-order and post-order, it is possible to construct the binary tree.

(h) A binary tree can be represented using array representation or linked representation.

(i) BST and AVL trees are special types of binary trees. They are created with an aim to improve the efficiency of working with binary trees.

(j) The property parent >= child is satisfied for all nodes in a max heap, and parent <= child for all nodes in a min heap.

Check Your Progress

Exercise - Level I

[A] State whether the following statements are True or False:

(a) A binary tree whose non-leaf nodes have left and the right child is a complete binary tree.

(b) The number of nodes attached to a particular node in a tree is called the degree of the node.

(c) To reconstruct a unique binary tree the in-order and pre-order lists are required.

(d) The balance factor of a node in an AVL tree is 1 if the height of the left sub-tree is one less than the height of the right sub-tree.

[B] Fill in the blanks:

(a) In a threaded binary tree the address of the in-order predecessor and in-order successor are stored in _____ and _____ child of the leaf node respectively.

(b) In any node of B-tree of order **n** the minimum required values and children are _____ and _____ respectively.

(c) In a heap if the largest element is present at the root node then it is called as the _____ heap.

Sharpen Your Skills

Exercise - Level II

[C] Answer the Following:

(a) Write a program that finds the height of a binary tree.

(b) Write a program that counts the number of nodes in a binary tree and the number of leaf nodes in a binary tree.

(c) Given a binary tree, create another binary tree that is mirror image of the given tree.

(d) Write a program that implements the non-recursive form of the functions **inorder( )**, **preorder( )** and **postorder( )**.

Coding Interview Questions

Exercise Level III

[D] Answer the Following:

(a) Given any number, write a program to find whether that number is present in the binary tree. If present then find the level at which it is present.

(b) Given two binary trees, write a program that finds whether
 − the two binary trees are similar
 − the two binary trees are mirror images of each other.

(c)   Write a program that finds the number of nodes in a binary tree at each level.

(d)   Write a program that traverses a binary tree level by level, from left towards right.

(e)   Write a function to insert a node **t** as a left child of any node **s** in a threaded binary tree.

Case Scenario Exercise

Dictionary implementation

We wish to maintain a dictionary of words as a binary tree. Each node should contain a word, its meaning, a synonym and an antonym. There must be a provision to insert a word, search a word and delete a word. It should be also possible to print the entire dictionary in alphabetical order.

08
Chapter

—

Graphs
Spread Your Tentacles

Why This Chapter Matters!

Networking! Be it any walk of life, that's the keyword today. Better your network, farther you would reach, and farther you spread your tentacles, better would be your network. And the crux of building and managing a network is hidden in a subject as innocuous as data structures in a topic called Graphs. Naturally, you must learn it to the best of your ability.

The only non-linear data structure that we have seen so far is tree. A tree in fact is a special type of graph. Graphs are data structures which have wide-ranging applications in real life. These include analysis of electrical circuits, finding shortest routes between cities, building a navigation system such as Google Maps, etc. To be able to understand and use the graph data structure one must first get familiar with the definitions and terms used in association with graphs. These are discussed below.

Definitions and Terminology

A graph consists of two sets **v** and **e,** where **v** is a finite, non-empty set of vertices and **e** is a set of pairs of vertices. The pairs of vertices are called edges. A Graph can be of two types: Undirected graph and Directed graph.

In an undirected graph the pair of vertices representing any edge is unordered. Thus, the pairs **(v1, v2)** and **(v2, v1)** represent the same edge.

In a directed graph each edge is represented by a directed pair **<v1, v2>**. **v1** is the tail and **v2** the head of the edge. Therefore, **<v2, v1>** and **<v1, v2>** represent two different edges. A directed graph is also called Digraph. In Figure 8-1 the graph **G1** is an undirected graph whereas graph **G2** is a directed graph.

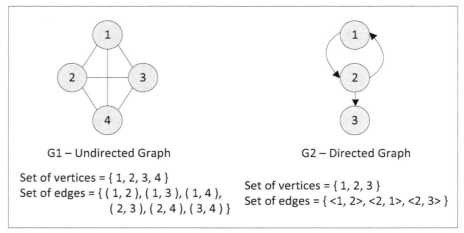

G1 – Undirected Graph

Set of vertices = { 1, 2, 3, 4 }
Set of edges = { (1, 2), (1, 3), (1, 4),
             (2, 3), (2, 4), (3, 4) }

G2 – Directed Graph

Set of vertices = { 1, 2, 3 }
Set of edges = { <1, 2>, <2, 1>, <2, 3> }

Figure 8-1. *Directed and undirected graphs.*

Note that the edges of a directed graph are drawn with an arrow from the tail to the head.

When Google Maps uses graph, each intersection is a vertex and each segment of road is an edge. Any useful information may be associated with both vertices and edges. For example, a navigation system could associate a GPS coordinate with each vertex and distance and speed limit with each edge.

Adjacent Vertices and Incident Edges

In an undirected graph if **(v1, v2)** is an edge in the set of edges, then the vertices **v1** and **v2** are said to be adjacent and the edge **(v1, v2)** is **incident on** vertices **v1** and **v2**. In Figure 8-2, vertex 2 in **G1** is **adjacent to** vertices 1, 3, and 4. The edges **incident on** vertex 3 in **G1** are **(1, 3)**, **(2, 3)** and **(4, 3)**.

If **<v1, v2>** is a directed edge, then vertex **v1** is said to be **adjacent to v2** while **v2** is **adjacent from v1**. The edge **<v1, v2>** is **incident on v1** and **v2**. In Figure 8-2, in **G2,** vertices 1 and 3 are **adjacent to** vertex 2, whereas, vertex 2 is **adjacent from** vertex 1. Also, the edges **incident on** vertex 2 are **<1 , 2>**, **< 2, 1 >** and **< 2, 3 >**.

Graph Representations

There are many ways of representing a graph in memory. Often, it will turn out that one of these representations will be better than others for a given application. The most commonly used representations for graphs are

(a) Adjacency matrix
(b) Adjacency lists
(c) Adjacency multi-lists

Each of these representations is discussed below.

Adjacency Matrix

An adjacency matrix of a graph is a 2-dimensional array of size **n x n** (where n is the number of vertices in the graph) with the property that **a[i][j] = 1** if the edge **(v$_i$, v$_j$)** is in the set of edges, and **a[i][j] = 0** if there is no such edge. The adjacency matrices for two sample graphs are shown in Figure 8-2.

As can be seen from Figure 8-2, the adjacency matrix for an undirected graph is symmetric. The adjacency matrix for a directed graph need not be symmetric. The space needed to represent a graph using its adjacency matrix is **n^2** locations. About half of this space can be saved in the case of undirected graphs by storing only the upper or lower triangle elements of the matrix.

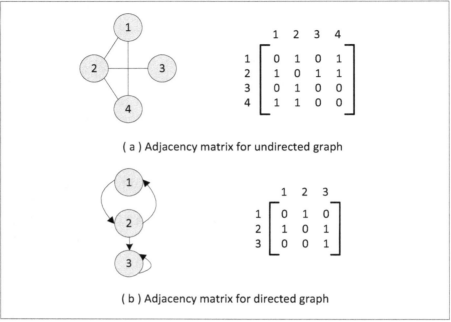

(a) Adjacency matrix for undirected graph

(b) Adjacency matrix for directed graph

Figure 8-2. *Adjacency matrices.*

Adjacency Lists

This is a vertex based-representation. In this representation we associate with each vertex a linked list of vertices adjacent to it. Normally an array is used to store the vertices. Each array element contains the vertex label, any other related information, plus a pointer to a linked list of nodes containing adjacent vertices. The array provides random access to the adjacency list for any particular vertex. The adjacency lists for two sample graphs are shown in Figure 8-3.

The advantage of this representation is that we can quickly find all the edges associated with a given vertex by traversing the list, instead of having to look through possibly hundreds of zero values to find a few ones in a row of an adjacency matrix.

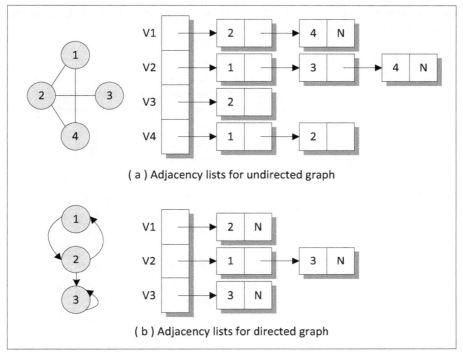

Figure 8-3. *Adjacency lists.*

In this representation, for an undirected graph each edge-information appears twice. For example, in Figure 8-3(a), vertex 1 and 2 are adjacent, hence vertex 2 appears in the list of vertex 1 and vertex 1 appears in the list of vertex 2.

Also, for a digraph it is easy to find the vertices adjacent to a given vertex. For example in Figure 8-3(b) to find vertices *adjacent to* vertex 2, we simply have to follow adjacency list of vertex 2. However, if we are to find out vertices *from* which to which 2 is *adjacent,* we have to scan the adjacency lists of all vertices. In Figure 8-3(b) on scanning all the lists, we can conclude that vertex 1 is the only vertex that is adjacent from vertex 2. This inefficiency related to a digraph can be rectified by using an adjacency multi-list representation.

Adjacency Multi-lists

An adjacency multi-list is an edge-based representation rather than a vertex-based representation. Each node that represents an edge consists of 5 fields. Of these, 2nd and 4th field are related and 3rd and 5th field are related. We would soon see the relationship.

Like adjacency list, an array of vertices is also maintained. Each array element points to a suitable edge node.

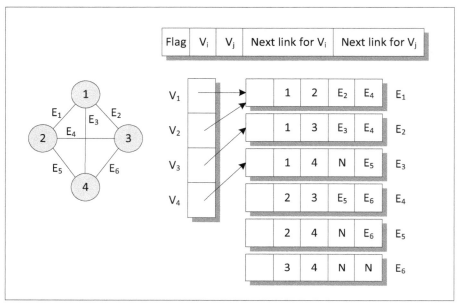

Figure 8-4. *Adjacency multi-lists for undirected graph.*

While constructing the multi-lists for graph shown in Figure 8-4 firstly the fields V_i and V_j are filled in the 6 edge nodes, E_1 to E_6. Then we start with vertex 1. This vertex has 3 incident edges E_1, E_2 and E_3. Hence the 1st element of vertices array is made to point to edge E_1. Then the edge node for E_1 is searched for vertex 1. It is found in V_i field of E_1. Since the next incident edge for vertex 1 is E_2 the fourth field of node E_1 is set up with pointer to edge node E_2. Then node E_2 is examined for vertex 1. Here also 1 is found in field V_i. Hence pointer to node E_3 is set up in fourth field of node E_2. Then E_3 is searched for vertex 1. It is found in field V_i. Since there are no more edges incident on vertex 1 hence fourth field of node E_3 is set with NULL.

Let us understand this process for vertex 2 as well. Vertex 2 has 3 incident edges E_1, E_4 and E_5. So to begin with, the 2nd element of vertices array is made to point to edge E_1. Then E_1 is searched for vertex 2. 1 is found in V_j field of E_1. Since the next incident edge for vertex 2 is E_4 the fifth field of node E_1 is set up with pointer to edge node E_4. Then node E_4 is examined for vertex 2. Here 2 is found in field V_i. Hence the fourth field of node E_4 is setup with pointer to edge E_5. Then E_5 is searched for vertex 2. It is found in field V_i. Since there are no more edges incident on vertex 2 hence fourth field of node E_5 is set with NULL.

If this procedure is carried out systematically for all other vertices then the adjacency multi-lists shown in Figure 8-4 would get created. If we traverse these lists for each element of the vertex array then we can find out the sequence of incident edges for each vertex. These sequences are given below.

Vertex 1 : E_1, E_2, E_3
Vertex 2 : E_1, E_4, E_5
Vertex 3 : E_2, E_4, E_6
Vertex 4 : E_3, E_5, E_6

On similar lines we can also create adjacency multi-lists for a directed graph. Only difference being, there would be two elements for each vertex in the array of vertices—one when the vertex is head of an edge and another when it is a tail. This is shown in Figure 8-5.

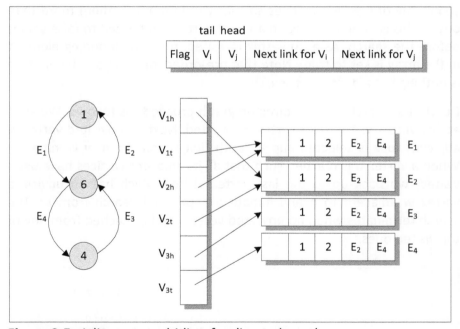

Figure 8-5. *Adjacency multi-lists for directed graph.*

If we traverse the lists shows in Figure 8-5 for each element of the vertex array, then we the sequence of incident edges for each vertex would be as follows. These sequences are given below.

V_{1h} : E_2
V_{1t} : E_1
V_{2h}: E_1, E_4

V_{2t} : E_2, E_3
V_{3h}: E_3
V_{3t} : E_4

Graph Traversals

Given the root node of a binary tree, one of the most common operations performed is visiting every node of the tree in some order. Similarly, given a vertex in a directed or undirected graph we may wish to visit all vertices in the graph that are reachable from this vertex. This can be done in two ways—using the Depth First Search and the Breadth First Search algorithm. Let us now understand these algorithms.

Depth First Search

In this algorithm we start at a vertex and move as far as we can down one path from the vertex before exploring the other paths. This requires some way of marking vertices so that we do not visit them more than once. This is done by using an array of vertices initialized to false values before the search. As each vertex is visited, the corresponding element in the array is set to true. Note that pre-order traversal of a binary tree is nothing but a depth first search.

Depth first search of an undirected graph proceeds as follows. We start at any vertex **v**. The start vertex **v** is visited. Next an unvisited vertex **w** adjacent to **v** is selected and a depth first search from **w** is initiated. When a vertex **u** is reached such that all its adjacent vertices have been visited, we back up to the last vertex visited which has an unvisited vertex **w** adjacent to it and initiate a depth first search from **w**. The search terminates when no unvisited vertex can be reached from any of the visited ones.

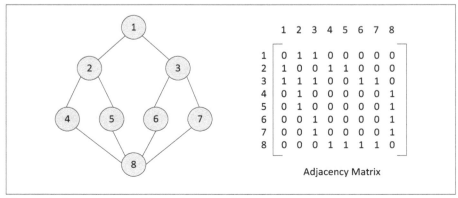

Figure 8-6. *Graph and its adjacency lists.*

Figure 8-6 shows a graph and its adjacency lists. If a depth first search is initiated from vertex **v₁**, then the vertices of this are visited in the order **V₁, V₂, V₄, V₈, V₅, V₆, V₃, V₇.**

The depth first search algorithm is implemented in the program given below.

Honest Solid Code

Program 8-1. Implementation of Depth First Search algorithm

```cpp
#include <iostream>
using namespace std ;

class graph
{
    private :

        int arr[ 8 ][ 8 ] ;
        int visited[ 8 ] ;

    public :

        graph( )
        {
            int i, j ;

            for ( i = 0 ; i < 8 ; i++ )
            {
                for ( j = 0 ; j < 8 ; j++ )
                    arr[ i ][ j ] = 0 ;
            }
            arr[ 0 ][ 1 ] = arr[ 1 ][ 0 ] = 1 ;
            arr[ 0 ][ 2 ] = arr[ 2 ][ 0 ] = 1 ;
            arr[ 1 ][ 3 ] = arr[ 3 ][ 1 ] = 1 ;
            arr[ 1 ][ 4 ] = arr[ 4 ][ 1 ] = 1 ;
            arr[ 2 ][ 5 ] = arr[ 5 ][ 2 ] = 1 ;
            arr[ 2 ][ 6 ] = arr[ 6 ][ 2 ] = 1 ;
            arr[ 3 ][ 7 ] = arr[ 7 ][ 3 ] = 1 ;
            arr[ 4 ][ 7 ] = arr[ 7 ][ 4 ] = 1 ;
            arr[ 5 ][ 7 ] = arr[ 7 ][ 5 ] = 1 ;
```

```
                    arr[ 6 ][ 7 ] = arr[ 7 ][ 6 ] = 1 ;

                    for ( i = 0 ; i < 8 ; i++ )
                        visited[ i ] = false ;
                }

                void dfs ( int sz, int idx )
                {
                    int  i ;

                    visited[ idx ] = 1 ;
                    cout << idx + 1 << " " ;

                    /* go to all columns of idx row */
                    for ( i = 0 ; i < sz ; i++ )
                    {
                        if ( visited[ i ] == 0 && arr[ idx ][ i ] == 1 )
                            dfs ( sz, i ) ;
                    }
                }
        } ;

        int main( )
        {
            graph g ;
            g.dfs ( 8, 0 ) ;
            return 0 ;
        }
```

Output:

```
1    2    4    8    5    6    3    7
```

The program uses adjacency matrix to create the graph shown in Figure 8-6. Once the matrix is created, the function **dfs( )** is called that visits each vertex and marks it as visited by storing a value in the **visited** array.

Breadth First Search

Starting at vertex **v** and marking it as visited, breadth first search differs from depth first search in that all unvisited vertices adjacent to **v**, are visited next. Then unvisited vertices adjacent to these vertices are visited and so on. A breadth first search beginning at vertex V_1 of graph shown in Figure 8-6 would first visit V_1 and then V_2 and V_3. Next vertices V_4, V_5, V_6 and V_7 will be visited and finally V_8.

Note that level-order traversal of a binary tree is nothing but breadth first search. The following program implements this algorithm.

Honest Solid Code

Program 8-2. Implementation of Breadth First Search algorithm

```cpp
#include <iostream>
using namespace std ;

const int MAX = 10 ;

class queue
{
    private :

        int  arr[ MAX ], front, rear ;

    public :

        queue( )
        {
            front = rear = -1 ;
        }

        /* adds an element to the queue */
        void addq ( int item )
        {
            if ( rear == MAX - 1 )
            {
                cout << "Queue is full" << endl ;
                return ;
            }

            rear++ ;
            arr[ rear ] = item ;

            if ( front == -1 )
```

```
                    front = 0 ;
          }

          /* removes an element from the queue */
          int delq( )
          {
              int data ;

              if ( front == -1 )
              {
                  cout << "Queue is Empty" << endl ;
                  return NULL ;
              }

              data = arr[ front ] ;
              arr[ front ] = 0 ;
              if ( front == rear )
                  front = rear = -1 ;
              else
                  front++ ;

              return  data ;
          }

          /* cheques whether queue is empty or not */
          bool isempty( )
          {
              if ( front == -1 && rear == -1 )
                  return true ;
              else
                  return false ;
          }
} ;

class graph
{
    private :

        int arr[ 8 ][ 8 ] ;
        int visited[ 8 ] ;
```

```
public :

    graph( )
    {
        int i, j ;

        for ( i = 0 ; i < 8 ; i++ )
        {
            for ( j = 0 ; j < 8 ; j++ )
                arr[ i ][ j ] = 0 ;
        }
        arr[ 0 ][ 1 ] = arr[ 1 ][ 0 ] = 1 ;
        arr[ 0 ][ 2 ] = arr[ 2 ][ 0 ] = 1 ;
        arr[ 1 ][ 3 ] = arr[ 3 ][ 1 ] = 1 ;
        arr[ 1 ][ 4 ] = arr[ 4 ][ 1 ] = 1 ;
        arr[ 2 ][ 5 ] = arr[ 5 ][ 2 ] = 1 ;
        arr[ 2 ][ 6 ] = arr[ 6 ][ 2 ] = 1 ;
        arr[ 3 ][ 7 ] = arr[ 7 ][ 3 ] = 1 ;
        arr[ 4 ][ 7 ] = arr[ 7 ][ 4 ] = 1 ;
        arr[ 5 ][ 7 ] = arr[ 7 ][ 5 ] = 1 ;
        arr[ 6 ][ 7 ] = arr[ 7 ][ 6 ] = 1 ;

        for ( i = 0 ; i < 8 ; i++ )
            visited[ i ] = false ;
    }

    void bfs ( int sz )
    {
        queue q ;
        int idx, i ;

        q.addq ( 0 ) ;
        while ( !q.isempty( ) )
        {
            idx = q.delq( ) ;
            if ( visited[ idx ] == 0 )
            {
                visited[ idx ] = 1 ;
                cout << idx + 1 << " " ;
                for ( i = 0 ; i < sz ; i++ )
                {
```

```
                              if ( visited[ i ] == 0 && arr[ idx ][ i ] == 1 )
                                  q.addq( i ) ;
                          }
                    }
                }
            }
};

int main( )
{
    graph g ;
    g.bfs ( 8 ) ;
    return 0 ;
}
```

Output:

1   2   3   4   5   6   7   8

The function **bfs( )** of the **graph** class visits each vertex and marks it visited. While doing so it uses the member functions **isempty( )**, **addq( )** and **delq( )** of the **queue** class to maintain a queue of vertices.

Spanning tree

A spanning tree of a graph is an undirected tree consisting of only those edges that are necessary to connect all the vertices in the original graph. Figure 8-7 shows a graph some of its spanning trees.

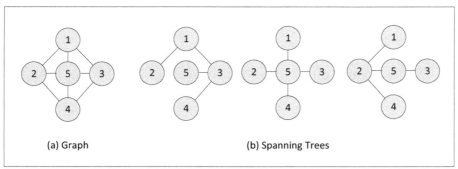

(a) Graph   (b) Spanning Trees

Figure 8-7. *Graph and its spanning trees.*

A spanning tree has a property that for any pair of vertices there exists only one path between them, and the insertion of any edge to a spanning tree form a unique cycle.

The particular spanning tree for a graph depends on the criteria used for generating it. The spanning tree resulting from a call to depth first tree is known as depth first spanning tree. Similarly, a spanning tree resulting from a call to breadth first tree is known as a breadth first spanning tree. Figure 8-8 shows a graph and its DFS and BFS spanning trees.

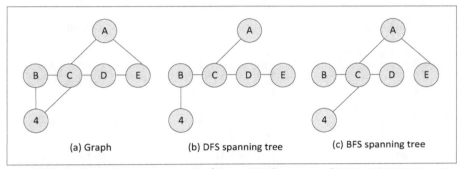

Figure 8-8. *Graph and its depth / breadth first search spanning tree.*

The spanning tree is useful in analysis of electrical circuits, shortest route problems and designing hydraulic / road / cable / computer network.

A graph may have weights on its edges. For example, if vertices A and B represent cities in a road network, then the weight on edge AB may represent cost of visiting B from A, or vice versa.

The cost of a spanning tree is the sum of costs of the edges in that tree. A minimum cost spanning tree has cost less than or equal to cost of all other spanning trees. Figure 8-9 shows a graph, its spanning trees and the minimum cost spanning tree.

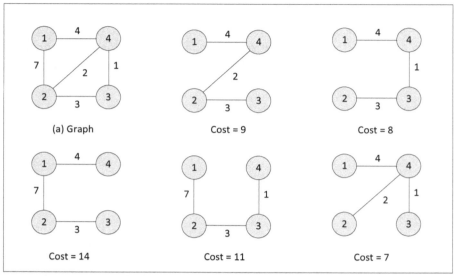

Figure 8-9. *Graph and its depth / breadth first search spanning tree.*

One method to determine a minimum cost spanning tree has been given by Kruskal. This method is discussed below.

Kruskal's Algorithm

In this algorithm a minimum cost spanning tree T is built edge by edge. Edges are considered for inclusion in T in increasing order of their costs. An edge is included in T if it does not form a cycle with edges already in T. Let us understand this with the help of an example.

Consider the graph shown in Figure 8-10. To find the minimum cost of spanning tree the edges are inserted into tree in increasing order of their costs. To begin with edge 4-3 is inserted as it has the lowest cost 1. Then the edge 4-2 is inserted which has a cost 2. The next edge in the order of cost is 3-2, but it is rejected as it forms a cyclic path between the vertices 2, 3 and 4. Then the edge 4-1 is inserted and it is accepted as it forms a non-cyclic path.

The minimum cost of spanning tree is given by the sum of costs of the existing edges, i.e. the edges that are inserted while building the spanning tree of minimum cost. In our case it is found to be 7.

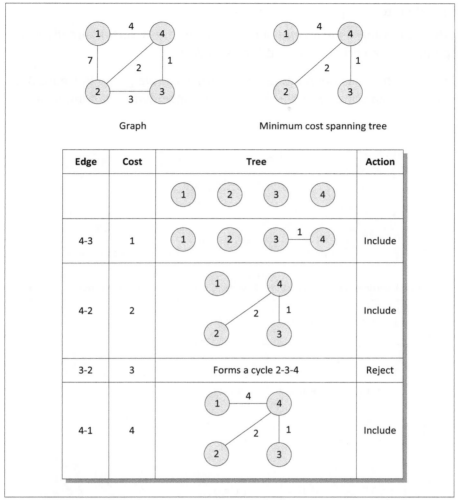

Figure 8-10. *Minimum cost spanning tree using Kruskal's algorithm.*

Prim's Algorithm

There is one more method to find the minimum cost spanning tree for a weighted undirected graph. This is known as Prim's algorithm. The steps involved in it are given below.

(a) Choose any vertex.
(b) Add it to the spanning tree vertex set and remove it from graph vertices set.
(c) Identify the vertices connected with the chosen vertex.
(d) Compare the weights of edges connecting the chosen vertex and identified vertices.
(e) Choose connected edge which has minimum weight.

(f) Add it to the spanning tree vertex set.

While choosing a vertex we should not choose a vertex already in the spanning tree vertex set or if it forms a cycle.

This algorithm has been implemented on a sample graph in Figure 8-11. The check mark indicates the vertex that is included after comparison.

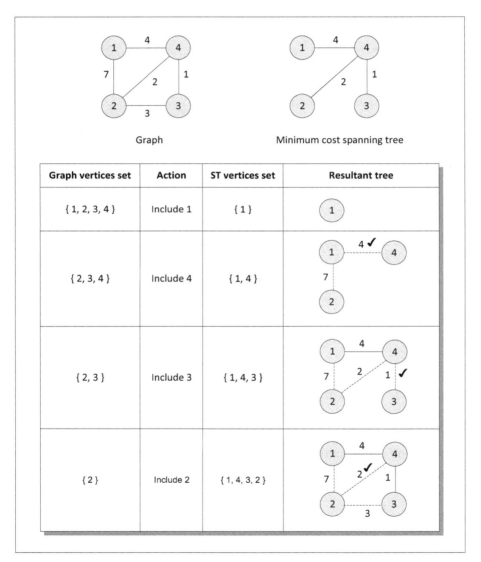

Figure 8-11. *Minimum cost spanning tree using Prim's algorithm.*

Shortest Path

A minimal spanning tree gives no indication about the shortest path between two nodes. Rather only the overall cost is minimized. In real life we are required to find shortest path between the two cities. For example, an airliner would be interested in finding most economical route between any two cities in a given network of cities. The algorithm to find such a path was first proposed by E.W.Dijkstra.

Dijkstra's Algorithm

This algorithm works for a directed as well as an undirected graph. Kruskal, Prim and Dijkstra algorithms are greedy algorithms. Typically, greedy algorithms build a solution piece by piece. At every step, they make a choice that looks best at that moment. Note that if a problem is solvable using greedy algorithm, it is usually the best solution.

The steps involved in Dijkstra's algorithm are given below.

(a) Mark all nodes as unvisited by creating a set of all the unvisited nodes.
(b) Assign distance values—0 to initial node, infinity to others.
(c) Set the initial node as current node and identify all of its unvisited neighbors.
(d) Calculate neighbor's distances from current node.
(e) Assign smaller of newly calculated and current distance.
(f) Mark the current node as visited.
(g) Set smallest distance unvisited node as new current node.
(h) Go back to step (c).

Dijkstra's algorithm can be best understood with the help of an example. Consider the weighted digraph shown in Figure 8-12. Let us begin with node 1 as the initial node. Set its distance value to 7 and distance value of other nodes to ∞. These values are shown in Figure 8-12 in boxes. Treat node 1 as the current node, so its neighbors will be nodes 2, 3 and 4. Recalculate the distance values by comparing existing values with actual distances and set the lower of the two. For example, current distance value of node 2 is ∞ and actual distance is 5. So lower of the two, i.e. 5 is set up as the new distance value. Distance values of nodes 3 and 4 would remain ∞ as there is no path from node 1 to nodes 3 and 4. Now mark node 1 as visited.

Next, compare the distances of nodes 2, 3 and 4 from node 1. They are 5, ∞ and ∞. Smallest amongst them is 5. So consider node 2 as the current node and repeat the same procedure again as shown in steps 3, 4 and 5 in Figure 8-12. Note that in step 3, cost of visiting node 4 from node 2 will be current cost + actual distance, i.e. 5 + 2 = 7. The final result of this process is shown in tabular form in Figure 8-11.

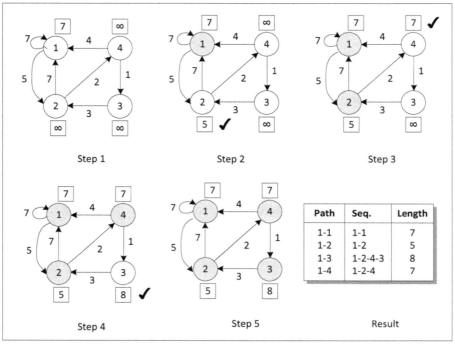

Figure 8-12. *Implementation of Dijkstra's algorithm.*

Note that we have found shortest path of all vertices from vertex 1. On similar lines, if we choose any other vertex as the starting vertex then we can find shortest distance of other vertices from the chosen vertex.

The following program shows how to find the shortest path between any two vertices.

Honest Solid Code   {C++}

Program 8-3. Implementation of Dijkstra's algorithm

```
#include <iostream>
using namespace std ;
```

```
const int INF = 999 ;

int main( )
{
    int arr[ 4 ][ 4 ] ;
    int cost[ 4 ][ 4 ] = {
                            7, 5, 0, 0,
                            7, 0, 0, 2,
                            0, 3, 0, 0,
                            4, 0, 1, 0
                        } ;
    int i, j, k, n = 4 ;

    for ( i = 0 ; i < n ; i++ )
    {
        for ( j = 0; j < n ; j++ )
        {
            if ( cost[ i ][ j ] == 0 )
                arr[ i ][ j ] = INF ;
            else
                arr[ i ][ j ] = cost[ i ][ j ] ;
        }
    }

    cout << "Adjacency matrix of cost of edges:" << endl ;
    for ( i = 0 ; i < n ; i++ )
    {
        for ( j = 0; j < n ; j++ )
            cout << arr[ i ][ j ] << "\t" ;

        cout << endl ;
    }

    for ( k = 0 ; k < n ; k++ )
    {
        for ( i = 0 ; i < n ; i++ )
        {
            for ( j = 0 ; j < n ; j++ )
            {
                if ( arr[ i ][ j ] > arr[ i ][ k ] + arr[ k ][ j ] )
                    arr[ i ][ j ] = arr[ i ][ k ] + arr[ k ][ j ];
```

```
            }
        }
    }

    cout << endl ;
    cout << "Adj. matrix of lowest cost between vertices:" << endl ;
    for ( i = 0 ; i < n ; i++ )
    {
        for ( j = 0; j < n ; j++ )
            cout << arr[ i ][ j ] << "\t" ;

        cout << endl ;
    }

    return 0 ;
}
```

Output:

Adjacency matrix of cost of edges:
```
7    5    999  999
7    999  999  2
999  3    999  999
4    999  1    999
```

Adj. matrix of lowest cost between vertices:
```
7    5    8    7
6    6    3    2
9    3    6    5
4    4    1    6
```

In the program the array **cost[ ]** is defined which is adjacency matrix of the cost of edges. In the array some values are 0 indicating that there is no direct path between the two vertices. One more array **arr[ ]** is defined which to begin with holds the value that the array **cost[ ]** holds. The only difference is instead of 0 it holds a value 999, which is defined as **INF** (infinity). Then through nested **for** loops the lowest value is assigned to each element of the array **arr[ ]** if the value already present is found to be greater.

Topological Sorting

Topological sorting is a special sorting technique that is relevant only for a Directed Acyclic Graph (DAG). If a DAG is represented using an array, then after sorting for every directed edge **uv**, **u** comes before **v** in the array. Note that for same DAG multiple solutions may exist.

Let us understand the sorting procedure using a sample DAG shown in Figure 8-13. We have to maintain a boolean array of vertices called **visited[ ]**. Initially, all elements of this array are set to false indicating that we haven't visited any vertices.

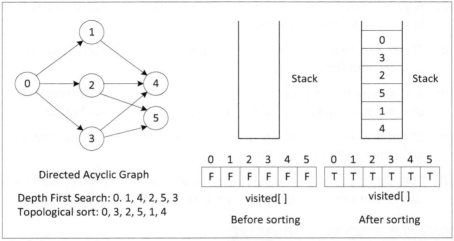

Figure 8-13. *Implementation of Topological sort*

Next, we have to start at a vertex with in-degree as 0, i.e. a vertex with no incoming edges. Suppose we start with vertex 0. So set value of **visited[0]** to true. From 0 we can go to 1, 2, or 3. Suppose we decide to visit 1. So set **visited[1]** to true. From 1 we can move further to 4, so set **visited[4]** to true. From 4 we cannot move any further, so we push 4 in a stack. Now go back to previous vertex, i.e. vertex 1. From 1 only vertex we can visit is 4 and it already stands visited. So push vertex 1 on the stack and go back to its previous vertex, i.e. 0. From 0 we can visit 1, 2 or 3. Of these, we have already visited 1, so let us now visit 2. Set **visited[2]** to true. From 2 we can visit either 4 or 5. But 5 has already been visited, so visit 5 and set **visited[4]** to true. Repeat this procedure till all vertices are visited. By that time the contents of the stack will be as shown in Figure 8-13. If we unwind the stack and print each element that is popped, we get the topological order of vertices. Confirm that in this order for every directed edge **uv**, **u** occurs before **v**.

Note that topological sorting is not same as DFS. As shown in Figure 8-13, the sequence of vertices of DFS and topological sort are different.

Chapter Bullets

Summary of chapter

(a) There are two types of graphs—directed graph and undirected graph.

(b) A graph can be represented using an adjacency matrix, adjacency lists or adjacency multi-lists.

(c) There are two algorithms for graph traversal—depth first search and breadth first search.

(d) A spanning tree is an undirected tree consisting of only those edges that are necessary to connect all vertices in the original graph.

(e) Minimum cost spanning tree can be obtained using Kruskal's algorithm or Prim's algorithm.

(f) The shortest path between vertices in a weighted directed graph can be obtained using Dijkstra's algorithm.

Check Your Progress

Exercise - Level I

[A] State whether the following statements are true or false:

(a) If **v1** and **v2** are two vertices of a directed graph **G**, then the edges **<v1, v2>** and **<v2, v1>** represent the same edge.

(b) For a graph there can exist only those many spanning trees as the number of vertices.

(c) To find minimum cost spanning tree edges are inserted in increasing order of their cost.

(d) The number of elements in the adjacency matrix of a graph having 6 vertices is 36.

(e) If V is the number of vertices and E is the number of edges in a graph, the time complexity to calculate the number of edges of the graph represented using an adjacency matrix is $O(V^2)$.

(f) If V is the number of vertices and E is the number of edges in a graph, time Complexity of Depth First Search is O(V + E).

(g) If V is the number of vertices and E is the number of edges in a graph, time Complexity of Breadth First Search is O(V + E).

(h) Adjacency matrix of any graph is always symmetric.

(i) Dijkstra's Algorithm works for both negative and positive weights.

Sharpen Your Skills

Exercise - Level II

[B] Choose the correct alternative for the following:

(a) For an adjacency matrix of a directed graph the row sum is the _____ degree of a vertex and the column sum is the _____ degree of the vertex.
 (1) in, out
 (2) out, in
 (3) in, total
 (4) total, out

(b) What is the maximum number of possible non-zero values in an adjacency matrix of a simple graph with n vertices?
 (1) (n * (n - 1)) / 2
 (2) (n * (n + 1)) / 2
 (3) n * (n - 1)
 (4) n * (n + 1)

(c) Breadth First Search is equivalent to which of the traversal in the Binary Trees?
 (1) Pre-order Traversal
 (2) Post-order Traversal
 (3) Level-order Traversal
 (4) In-order Traversal

(d) Depth First Search is equivalent to which binary tree traversal?
 (1) Pre-order Traversal
 (2) Post-order Traversal

(3) Level-order Traversal

(4) In-order Traversal

(e) The data structure used in implementation of Breadth First Search is

(1) Stack

(2) Queue

(3) Linked List

(4) None of the mentioned

(f) The data structure used in implementation of Breadth First Search is?

(1) Stack

(2) Queue

(3) Linked List

(4) None of the mentioned

(g) Joshi wants to visit 5 cities starting from Mumbai with an aim to minimize the cost of travel. Which of the following algorithm should he use?

(1) Depth First Search

(2) Kruskal's algorithm

(3) Prim's algorithm

(4) Dijkstra's algorithm

Coding Interview Questions

Exercise Level III

[C] Answer the following:

(a) If a graph is represented using an adjacency matrix, write a program that finds

— the number of vertices in a graph.

— the number of adjacent vertices for a given vertex.

(b) What would be the sequence of nodes if the graph shown is Figure 8-14(a) is traversed using DFS algorithm starting at vertex 6?

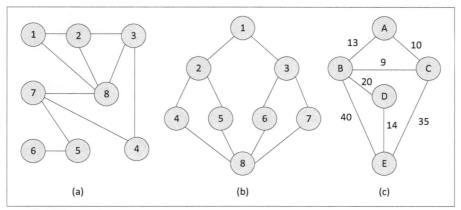

Figure 8-14. *Graphs.*

(c) What would be the sequence of nodes if the graph shown is Figure 8-14(b) is traversed using BFS algorithm starting at vertex 5?

(d) Create a minimum spanning tree for graph shown in Figure 8-14(c) using Kruskal's algorithm.

(e) Create a minimum spanning tree for graph shown in Figure 8-14(c) using Prim's algorithm.

Case Scenario Exercise

Kruskal's and Prim's algorithm

Write a program to implement Kruskal's and Prim's algorithms. Also analyze the time complexity of each implementation.

09
Chapter

—

Searching and Sorting
Seek Me Out, Sort Me Out

Why This Chapter Matters?

It would be an interesting statistic to find out how much time pre-computer-age generations spent in searching things and arranging them in an order. What a colossal waste it must have been to do these things manually! When history of computing is written 'searching' and 'sorting' would be right there at the top, as entities responsible for changing the way people do work.

245

We often spend time in searching some thing or the other. If the data is kept properly in some sorted order then searching becomes very easy. Think of searching a word's meaning from an unordered list of words and then you will appreciate the way a dictionary is designed. In this chapter we are going to discuss different types of searching and sorting methods. Let us start with searching methods.

Searching

Searching is an operation that finds the location of a given element in a list. The search is said to be successful or unsuccessful depending on whether the element that is to be searched is found or not. Here, we will discuss two standard searching methods—Linear search and Binary search.

Linear Search

This is the simplest method of searching. In this method, an element is searched in the list sequentially. This method can be applied to a sorted or an unsorted list. Searching in unsorted list starts from the 0th element and continues until the element is found or the end of list is reached. As against this, searching in an ascending order sorted list starts from 0th element and continues until the element is found or an element whose value is greater than the value being searched is reached.

Following program implements linear search method for an unsorted as well as a sorted array.

Honest Solid Code

Program 9-1. Implementation of Linear Search algorithm

```
#include <iostream>
using namespace std ;

int searchinsorted ( int [ ], int, int ) ;
int searchinunsorted ( int [ ], int, int ) ;

int main( )
{
    int unsortedarr[ 10 ] = { 11, 2, 9, 13, 57, 25, 17, 1, 90, 3 } ;
```

```
    int sortedarr[ 10 ] = { 1, 2, 3, 9, 11, 13, 17, 25, 57, 90 } ;
    int num, pos ;

    cout << "Enter number to search: " ;
    cin >> num ;
    pos = searchinunsorted ( unsortedarr, 10, num ) ;
    if ( pos == -1 )
        cout << "Number is not present in the array" << endl ;
    else
        cout << "Number is at position " << pos << " in array" << endl ;

    printf ( "Enter number to search: " ) ;
    cin >> num ;
    pos = searchinunsorted ( sortedarr, 10, num ) ;
    if ( pos == -1 )
        cout << "Number is not present in the array" << endl ;
    else
        cout << "Number is at position " << pos << " in array" << endl ;

    return 0 ;
}

int searchinunsorted ( int arr[ ], int size, int num )
{
    int i ;

    for ( i = 0 ; i < size ; i++ )
    {
        if ( arr[ i ] == num )
            return i ;
    }

    return -1 ;
}

int searchinsorted ( int arr[ ], int size, int num )
{
    int i ;

    if ( num > arr[ size - 1 ] )
        return -1 ;
```

```
    for ( i = 0 ; i < size ; i++ )
    {
        if ( arr[ i ] > num )
            return -1 ;

        if ( arr[ i ] == num )
            return i ;
    }
    return -1 ;
}
```

Output:

Enter number to search: 13
Number is at position 3 in the array
Enter number to search: 100
Number is not present in the array

In the program, **num** is the number that is to be searched in the array. While searching in **unsortedarr**, inside the **for** loop each time **arr[i]** is compared with **num**. If any element is equal to **num**, it means that the element is found. Hence its position in the array is returned. If control reaches beyond the **for** loop, it means that the element is not present in the array. In this case -1 is returned. We have returned -1, because no element can be present at position -1 in the array.

While searching in a sorted array, search starts at the 0th element and ends when the element is found or any element of the list is found to be greater than the element to be searched.

The number of comparisons in case of sorted list might be less as compared to the unsorted list because the search may not always continue till the end of the list.

The performance of linear search algorithm can be measured by counting the number of comparisons done to locate an element. In the worst case, in an array of size **n**, this algorithm would carry out **n** comparisons to reach a conclusion whether the element being searched is present in the array or not. Hence worst case time complexity of this algorithm is **O (n)**.

Binary Search

Binary search method is very fast and efficient. This method requires that the list of elements be in sorted order. In this method, to search an element we compare it with the element present at the center of the list. If it matches then the search is successful. Otherwise, the list is divided into two halves—one from 0th element to the center element (first half), and another from center element to the last element (second half). As a result, all the elements in first half are smaller than the center element, whereas, all the elements in second half are greater than the center element.

The searching will now proceed in first or second half depending upon whether the element is smaller or greater than the center element. Same process of comparing the required element with the center element and if not found then dividing the elements into two halves is repeated for the first half or second half. This procedure is repeated till the element is found or the division of half parts gives one element. Let us understand this with the help of Figure 9-1.

				arr[ ]						num
1	2	3	9	11	13	17	25	57	90	57
1	2	3	9	11	13	17	25	57	90	57
1	2	3	9	11	13	17	25	57	90	57

Figure 9-1. *Binary search.*

Suppose an array consists of 10 sorted numbers and 57 is element that is to be searched. The binary search method when applied to this array works as follows:

(a) 57 is compared with the element present at the center of the list (i.e. 11). Since 57 is greater than 11, the searching is restricted only to the second half of the array.

(b) Now 57 is compared with the center element of the second half of array (i.e. 25). Here again 57 is greater than 25 so the searching now proceeds in the elements present between 25 and 90.

(c) This process is repeated till 57 is found or no further division of sub-array is possible.

Following program implements the binary search algorithm.

Honest Solid Code   {C++}

Program 9-2. Implementation of Binary Search algorithm

```
#include <iostream>
using namespace std ;

int binarysearch ( int [ ], int, int ) ;

int main( )
{
    int arr[ ] = { 1, 2, 3, 9, 11, 13, 17, 25, 57, 90 } ;
    int num, pos ;

    cout << "Enter number to search: " ;
    cin >> num ;
    pos = binarysearch ( arr, 10, num ) ;
    if ( pos == -1 )
        cout << "Number is not present in the array" << endl ;
    else
        cout << "Number is at position " << pos << " in array" << endl ;

    return 0 ;
}

int binarysearch ( int a[ ], int size, int num )
{
    int  lower, upper, mid ;

    lower = 0 ;
    upper = size ;

    while ( lower <= upper )
    {
        mid = ( lower + upper ) / 2 ;
        if ( num == a[ mid ] )
            return mid ;
        if ( num > a[ mid ] )
```

```
            lower = mid + 1 ;
        if ( num < a[ mid ] )
            upper = mid - 1 ;
    }

    return -1 ;
}
```

Output:

Enter number to search: 57
Number is at position 8 in the array

In 1st iteration the algorithm works with n elements

In 2nd iteration it works with n / 2 elements

In 3rd iteration it works with (n / 2) / 2 elements

In 4th iteration it works with ((n / 2) / 2) / 2 elements

This goes on till we reach an iteration where number of elements being worked upon becomes 1. Suppose **k** iterations would be required to reach input size of 1. Thus,

$n / 2^k = 1$

Taking log of both sides we get,

$\log_2 2^k = \log_2 n$

Therefore, $k = \log_2 n$.

During each iteration maximum of 3 comparisons are done. Thus number of comparisons in binary search is limited to 3 * **$\log_2$ n**. Ignoring the constant 3, the time complexity will be **O ($\log_2$ n)**.

Thus a binary search gives better performance than linear search. The disadvantage of binary search is that it works only on sorted lists. So if searching is to be performed on an unsorted list then linear search is the only option.

Recursive Binary Search

We have used a **while** loop to implement the binary search algorithm in Program 9-2. It is also possible to implement this algorithm using recursion. This recursive implementation is given below.

Honest Solid Code

{C++}

Program 9-3. Implementation of Recursive Binary Search algorithm

```cpp
#include <iostream>
using namespace std ;

int recbinsearch ( int [ ], int, int, int ) ;

int main( )
{
    int arr[ ] = { 1, 2, 3, 9, 11, 13, 17, 25, 57, 90 } ;
    int num, pos ;

    cout << "Enter number to search: " ;
    cin >> num ;
    pos = recbinsearch ( arr, num, 0, 10 ) ;
    if ( pos == -1 )
        cout << "Number is not present in the array" << endl ;
    else
        cout << "Number is at position " << pos << " in array" << endl ;

    return 0 ;
}

int recbinsearch ( int  a[ ], int  num, int  lower, int upper )
{
        int mid ;

        if ( lower <= upper )
        {
            mid = ( lower + upper ) / 2 ;
            if ( num == a[ mid ] )
                return mid ;
            if ( num > a[ mid ] )
                lower = mid + 1 ;
            if ( num < a[ mid ] )
                upper = mid - 1 ;

            return recbinsearch ( a, num, lower, upper ) ;
```

```
        }

    return -1 ;
}
```

In **recbinsearch( )** we compare **num** with the middle element. If it matches with middle element, we return the index mid. Otherwise if **num** is found to be greater than the mid element, then **num** can only lie in right half subarray after the mid element. So we call **recbinsearch( )** for right half of the array. Finally, if **num** is found to be smaller than the mid element, then **num** can only lie in left half subarray before the mid element. So we call **recbinsearch( )** for left half of the array.

To find time complexity of recursive binary search algorithm, let us consider 3 cases shown in Figure 9-2.

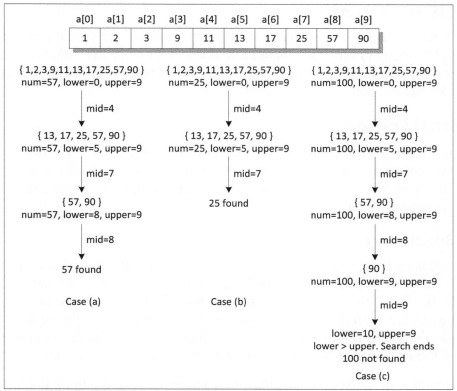

Figure 9-2. *Progress of recursive Binary search.*

In case (a) it takes 3 comparisons to search 57. In case (b) it takes 2 comparisons to search 25. Lastly, in case (c), it takes 4 comparisons to reach a conclusion that 100 in not present in the array. So, we can conclude that, in worst case, it does **log₂ n** comparisons. Note that value of log₂ 10 is between 3 and 4. To get exact number of comparisons the input array size must be a power of 2. We can safely conclude that that the time complexity of recursive binary search algorithm is O (**log₂ n)**.

Sorting

Sorting refers to arranging elements of a set in some order. There are different methods that are used to sort the data in ascending or descending order. These methods can be divided into two categories. They are as follows:

Internal Sorting

If all the data to be sorted can be accommodated at a time in memory then internal sorting methods are used.

External Sorting

When the data to be sorted is so large that some of the data is present in the memory and some is kept in auxiliary memory (hard disk, tape, etc.), then external sorting methods are used. Let us begin with internal sorting methods.

Internal Sorting

There are different types of internal sorting algorithms. We will discuss the common algorithms here. These algorithms sort the data is ascending order. With a minor change we can also sort the data in descending order.

Bubble Sort

In this method, firstly 0th and 1st elements are compared. If 0th element is found to be greater than the 1st element then they are interchanged. Next, the 1st element is compared with the 2nd element, if it is found to be greater, then they are interchanged. In the same way all the adjacent pairs of elements are compared and interchanged if required. At the end of this iteration the largest element gets placed at the last position.

Similarly, in the second iteration the comparisons are made till the last but one element and this time the second largest element gets placed at the second last position in the list.

Once all such iterations are completed the list becomes a sorted list. This can be easily understood with the help of Figure 9-3.

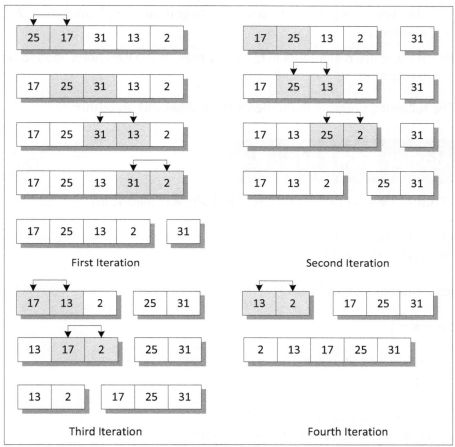

Figure 9-3. *Bubble sort at work.*

Suppose an array **arr** consists of 5 numbers. The bubble sort algorithm works as follows:

(a) In the first iteration the 0th element 25 is compared with 1st element 17 and since 25 is greater than 17, they are interchanged.

(b) Now the 1st element 25 is compared with 2nd element 31. But 25 is less than 31, so are not interchanged.

(c) This process is repeated until $(n - 2)^{nd}$ element is compared with $(n - 1)^{th}$ element and interchanged if required.

(d) At the end of the first iteration, the $(n - 1)^{th}$ element holds the largest number.

(e) Now the second iteration starts with the 0th element 17. The above process of comparison and interchanging is repeated but this time the last comparison is made between $(n - 3)^{rd}$ and $(n - 2)^{nd}$ elements.

(f)   If there are n elements in the array then (n - 1) iterations need to be performed.

The following program implements the bubble sort algorithm.

Honest Solid Code   {C++}

Program 9-4. Implementation of Bubble Sort algorithm

```cpp
#include <iostream>
using namespace std ;

void bubblesort ( int [ ], int ) ;

int main( )
{
    int arr[ ] = { 25, 17, 31, 13, 2 } ;
    int i ;

    cout << "Bubble sort" << endl ;
    cout << "Array before sorting:" << endl ;
    for ( i = 0 ; i < 5 ; i++ )
        cout << arr[ i ] << "\t" ;

    bubblesort ( arr, 5 ) ;

    cout << endl << "Array after sorting:" << endl ;
    for ( i = 0 ; i < 5 ; i++ )
        cout << arr[ i ] << "\t" ;

    return 0 ;
}

void bubblesort ( int a[ ], int size )
{
    int i, j, temp ;

    for ( i = 0 ; i < size - 1 ; i++ )
```

```
    {
        for ( j = 0 ; j < size - i - 1 ; j++ )
        {
            if ( a[ j ] > a[ j + 1 ] )
            {
                temp = a[ j ] ;
                a[ j ] = a[ j + 1 ] ;
                a[ j + 1 ] = temp ;
            }
        }
    }
}
```

Output:

Bubble sort
Array before sorting:
25   17   31   13   2
Array after sorting:
2   13   17   25   31

The elements compared in bubble sort are always adjacent. Hence each time the elements compared are **a[j]** and **a[j + 1]**. If the element **a[j]** is found to be greater than **a[j + 1]** then they are interchanged.

If we wish to arrange the numbers in descending order then we need to make a small change in the condition, as shown below:

```
if ( a[ j ] < a[ j + 1 ] )
{
    /*  exchange a[ j ] with a[ j + 1 ]  */
}
```

When the array has 5 elements the number of comparisons that would be made in each iteration would be as follows:

1st iteration - 4 comparisons
2nd iteration - 3 comparisons
3rd iteration - 2 comparisons
4th iteration - 1 comparison

So, in general, for an array of **n** elements the number of comparisons will be **n (n - 1) / 2**. So time complexity of selection sort algorithm is **O (n^2)**.

Selection Sort

This is perhaps the simplest method of sorting. In this method, to sort the data in ascending order, the 0th element is compared with all other elements. If the 0th element is found to be greater than the compared element then they are interchanged. So after the first iteration the smallest element gets placed at the 0th position. The same procedure is repeated for the 1st element and so on. This procedure can be best understood with the help of Figure 9-4.

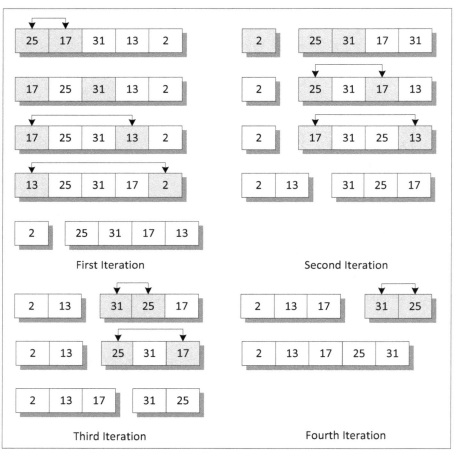

Figure 9-4. *Selection sort at work.*

Suppose an array **arr** consists of 5 numbers. The selection sort algorithm works as follows:

(a) In the first iteration the 0th element 25 is compared with 1st element 17 and since 25 is greater than 17, they are interchanged.

(d) Now the 0th element 17 is compared with 2nd element 31. But 17 is less than 31, so are not interchanged.

(e) This process is repeated till 0th element is compared with rest of the elements and interchanged if necessary.

(f) At the end of the first iteration, the 0th element is the smallest element.

(g) Now the second iteration starts with the 1st element 25. The above process of comparison and swapping is repeated.

(h) So if there are n elements in the array, then after (n - 1) iterations the array is sorted.

The following program sorts the given list using selection sort algorithm.

Honest Solid Code   {C++}

Program 9-5. Implementation of Selection Sort algorithm

```cpp
#include <iostream>
using namespace std ;

void selectionsort ( int [ ], int ) ;

int main( )
{
    int arr[ ] = { 25, 17, 31, 13, 2 } ;
    int i ;

    cout << "Selection sort" << endl ;
    cout << "Array before sorting:" << endl ;
    for ( i = 0 ; i < 5 ; i++ )
        cout << arr[ i ] << "\t" ;

    selectionsort ( arr, 5 ) ;

    cout << endl << "Array after sorting:" << endl ;
    for ( i = 0 ; i < 5 ; i++ )
        cout << arr[ i ] << "\t" ;

    return 0 ;
```

```
}

void selectionsort ( int a[ ], int size )
{
    int i, j, temp ;

    for ( i = 0 ; i < size - 1 ; i++ )
    {
        for ( j = i + 1 ; j < size ; j++ )
        {
            if ( a[ i ] > a[ j ] )
            {
                temp = a[ i ] ;
                a[ i ] = a[ j ] ;
                a[ j ] = temp ;
            }
        }
    }
}
```

Output:

Selection sort
Array before sorting:
25   17   31   13   2
Array after sorting:
2   13   17   25   31

Here, **a[i]** is compared with **a[j]**. If the element **a[i]** is found to be greater than **a[j]** then they are interchanged. The value of **j** is starting from **i + 1**, as we need to compare any element with all elements following it.

When the array has 5 elements the number of comparisons made in each iteration will be as follows:

1st iteration - 4 comparisons
2nd iteration - 3 comparisons
3rd iteration - 2 comparisons
4th iteration - 1 comparison

So, in general, for an array of **n** elements the number of comparisons will be **n (n - 1) / 2**. So time complexity of selection sort algorithm is **O (n^2)**.

Insertion Sort

This algorithm works by inserting each element at an appropriate position in the array. The array is divided into two sets—one contains sorted values and another contains unsorted values. To begin with, the element at 0th position is in the sorted set and the rest are in the unsorted set. During each iteration, the first element in the unsorted set is picked up and inserted at the correct position in the sorted set. The correct position is determined by traversing the sorted set from right to left and comparing the picked element with the elements in the sorted set. During comparison if it is found that picked element can be inserted then space is created for it by shifting the other elements one position to the right. Let us understand this algorithm with the help of Figure 9-5.

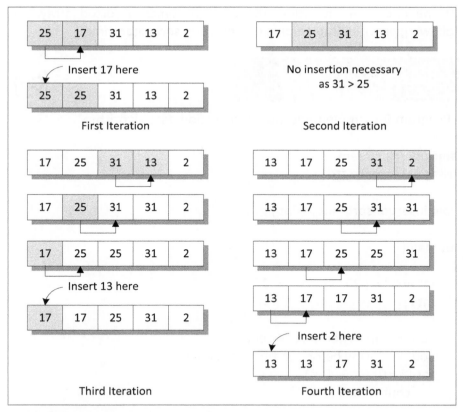

Figure 9-5. *Insertion sort at work.*

Given below is the explanation of insertion sort algorithm for an array of 5 elements shown in Figure 9-5:

(a) In the first iteration the 1st element 17 is compared with the 0th element 25. Since 17 is smaller than 25, 17 is inserted at 0th place. Before that the 0th element 25 is shifted one position to the right.

(b) In the second iteration, the 2nd element 31 is compared with element before it, i.e. 25. Since 31 is greater than 25, nothing is done as 31 is at its correct position.

(c) In the third iteration, the 3rd element 13 is compared successively with 31, 25, and 17. Since, 13 is smaller than all of them, they are shifted to right by one position and then 13 is inserted.

(d) In the fourth iteration the 4th element 2 is compared with elements 31, 25, 17 and 13. Since, 2 is smaller than all of them, these elements are shifted to right by one position and then 2 is inserted.

At the end of 4th iteration, the array becomes a sorted array. The following program implements the insertion sort algorithm:

Honest Solid Code   {C++}

Program 9-6. Implementation of Insertion Sort algorithm

```
#include <iostream>
using namespace std ;

void insertionsort ( int [ ], int ) ;

int main( )
{
    int arr[ ] = { 25, 17, 31, 13, 2 } ;
    int i ;

    cout << "Insertion sort" << endl ;
    cout << "Array before sorting:" << endl ;
    for ( i = 0 ; i < 5 ; i++ )
        cout << arr[ i ] << "\t" ;

    insertionsort ( arr, 5 ) ;

    cout << endl << "Array after sorting:" << endl ;
    for ( i = 0 ; i < 5 ; i++ )
        cout << arr[ i ] << "\t" ;
```

```
        return 0 ;
}

void insertionsort ( int a[ ], int size )
{
    int i, j, k, temp ;

    for ( i = 1 ; i < size ; i++ )
    {
        temp = a[ i ] ;
        j = i - 1 ;
        while ( j >= 0 && a[ j ] > temp )
        {
            a[ j + 1 ] = a[ j ] ;
            j-- ;
        }

        a[ j + 1 ] = temp ;
    }
}
```

Output:

Insertion sort
Array before sorting:
25   17   31   13   2
Array after sorting:
2   13   17   25   31

In the program the outer **for** loop is starting from 1 as the unsorted set starts at 1st position. The inner loop is used for comparison to decide the position where the picked element (**temp**) and for shifting the elements one position to the right to make room for inserting the picked element.

Let us consider best case and worst case for analyzing the time complexity of this algorithm. The best case is when the array is already sorted and the worst case is when the array elements are in descending order. The important operations to be considered in this algorithm are comparison to determine where the element should be inserted and movement to create space for inserting the element.

In the best case the number of comparisons and movements will be as shown below.

for i = 1, 1 comparison + 0 movement = 1
for i = 2, 1 comparison + 0 movement = 1
for i = 3, 1 comparison + 0 movement = 1
for i = 4, 1 comparison + 0 movement = 1
...
...
for i = n, 1 comparison + 0 movement = 1

So total number of operations will be 1 + 1 + 1 + 1.... This sum will be equal to **n**. Thus time complexity in best case will be **O (n)**.

In the worst case the number of comparisons and movements will be as shown below.

for i = 2, 1 comparison + 1 movement = 2
for i = 3, 2 comparisons + 2 movements = 4
for i = 3, 3 comparisons + 3 movements = 6
for i = 4, 3 comparisons + 3 movements = 8
for i = n, n - 1 comparisons + n - 1 movements= 2(n - 1)

If we add all this, we get

$$2 + 4 + 6 + 8 + ... + 2 (n - 1)$$
$$= 2 (1 + 2 + 3 + + 4... + (n - 1))$$
$$= 2 (n (n - 1) / 2)$$
$$= O (n^2)$$

Thus time complexity in best case will be **O (n²)**.

Quick Sort

Quick sort is a very popular sorting method. It is also known as **partition exchange sort**. The basis of this algorithm is that it is faster and easier to sort two small arrays than one large array. Thus the basic strategy of quick sort is to divide and conquer.

Consider a stack of papers each bearing name of a student and we wish to sort them by name. We can use the following approach. Pick a splitting value, say L (known as **pivot** element) and divide the stack of papers into two piles, A-L and M-Z (note that each pile may not contain the same number of papers). Then take the first pile and sub-divide it into two piles, A-F and G-L. The A-F pile can be further broken down into A-C and D-F. This division process goes on until the piles are small enough to be easily sorted. The same process is applied to the M-Z pile.

Eventually, all the small sorted piles can be stacked one on top of the other to produce an ordered set of papers.

This strategy is based on recursion—on each attempt to sort the stack of papers, the pile is divided and then the same approach is used to sort each smaller pile (a smaller case).

The quick sort algorithm can be explained with the help of Figure 9-6. In this figure the element marked by '*' is the pivot element and the element marked by '—' is the element whose position is finalized.

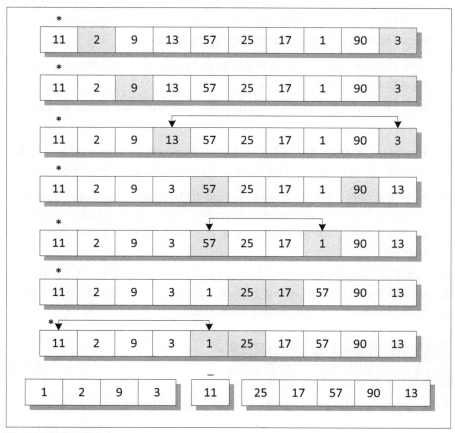

Figure 9-6. *Quick sort.*

The array in Figure 9-6 consists of 10 elements. The quick sort algorithm works as follows:

(a) In the first iteration, we take the 0th element, i.e. 11, as a pivot element and place it at its final position such that all elements to the left of it are less than 11 and all elements to the right of it are greater than 11. To divide the array in this way we use two index variables, **p** and **q**.

(b) Using index variable **p** we move in the array from left to right in search of an element greater than 11. In our case **p** is incremented till we reach 13.

(c) Similarly, using **q** we move in the array from right to left in search of an element smaller than 11. In our case **q** is not decremented even once because 3 is less than 11.

(d) Now 13 and 3 are interchanged. Again, from their current positions **p** and **q** are incremented and decremented respectively and exchanges are made appropriately if desired.

(e) The process ends when **p** exceeds **q**. In our case, this happens when **p** reaches 25 and **q** reaches 1.

(f) Now, the 0th element 11 is interchanged with the value at index **q**, i.e. 1.

(g) The array is thus divided into two sub-arrays—elements to the left of 11 and elements to the right of 11, with 11 at its final position.

(h) Now the same procedure is applied to the two sub-arrays and then to the sub-arrays of these sub-arrays. As a result, at the end when all sub-arrays contain only one element, the original array gets sorted.

Note that it is not necessary that the pivot element must be the 0th element. We can choose any other element as pivot. The program given below implements the quick sort algorithm.

Honest Solid Code   {C++}

Program 9-7. Implementation of Quick Sort algorithm

```
#include <iostream>
using namespace std ;

void quicksort ( int [ ], int, int ) ;
int split ( int [ ], int, int ) ;

int main( )
{
```

```
    int arr[ ] = { 11, 2, 9, 13, 57, 25, 17, 1, 90, 3 } ;
    int i ;

    cout << "Quick sort" << endl ;
    cout << "Array before sorting:" << endl ;
    for ( i = 0 ; i < 10 ; i++ )
        cout << arr[ i ] << "\t" ;

    quicksort ( arr, 0, 9 ) ;

    cout << endl << "Array after sorting:" << endl ;
    for ( i = 0 ; i < 10 ; i++ )
        cout << arr[ i ] << "\t" ;

    return 0 ;
}

void quicksort ( int a[ ], int lower, int upper )
{
    int i ;

    if ( upper > lower )
    {
        i = split ( a, lower, upper ) ;
        quicksort ( a, lower, i - 1 ) ;
        quicksort ( a, i + 1, upper ) ;
    }
}

int split ( int a[ ], int lower, int upper )
{
    int p, q, num, temp ;

    p = lower + 1 ;
    q = upper ;
    num = a[ lower ] ;

    while ( q >= p )
    {
        while ( a[ p ] < num )
            p++ ;
```

```
        while ( a[ q ] > num )
            q-- ;

        if ( q > p )
        {
            temp = a[ p ] ;
            a[ p ] = a[ q ] ;
            a[ q ] = temp ;
        }
    }

    temp = a[ lower ] ;
    a[ lower ] = a[ q ] ;
    a[ q ] = temp ;

    return q ;
}
```

Output:

Quick sort
Array before sorting:
11   2   9   13   57   25   17   1   90   3
Array after sorting:
1   2   3   9   11   13   17   25   57   90

The first and last indexes passed to **quicksort( )** reflect the part of the array that is being currently processed. In the first call we pass 0 and 9, since there are 10 integers in our array.

In the function **quicksort( )**, a condition is checked whether **upper** is greater than **lower**. If the condition is satisfied then only the array will be split into two parts, otherwise, the control will simply be returned. To split the array into two parts the function **split( )** is called.

In the function **split( )**, to start with the two variables **p** and **q** are assigned the values **lower + 1** and **upper**. Then a **while** loop is executed that checks whether the indexes **p** and **q** have crossed each other. If they haven't then inside the **while** loop two more nested **while** loops are executed to increase the index **p** and decrease the index **q**. Then it is checked whether **q** is greater than **p**. If so, then the elements present at **p**[th] and **q**[th] positions are interchanged.

Finally, when the control returns to the function **quicksort( )** two recursive calls are made to function **quicksort( )**. This is done to sort the two split sub-arrays. As a result, after all the recursive calls when the control reaches the function **main( )** the arrays becomes sorted.

In quick sort we choose a pivot and then split the array into sub-arrays. Then we again choose a pivot element in each of these sub-arrays and further split them. The best case in quick sort would be when we always choose the middle element of the array as the pivot element. Suppose to reach a sub-array of 1 element we have to do **k** iterations.

Then, $n / 2^k = 1$.

Taking log of both sides we get,

$\log_2 2^k = \log_2 n$

Therefore, $k = \log_2 n$.

In each of these **k** iterations for splitting the array we have to do **n** comparisons. Hence the total number of comparisons in quick sort will be **n * $\log_2$ n**. So time complexity of quick sort in best case is **O ($\log_2$ n)**.

The worst case in quick sort will occur when the input is an array which is already sorted. In this case if we take the first element as pivot then there won't be any left sub-array. Except the pivot, all elements will be in right sub-array. Same thing will happen at each level. So while splitting there will be **n** comparisons at level 1, **n - 1** comparison at level 2, n - 3 comparisons at level 3, etc. So totally there will be **n * (n + 1) / 2** comparisons. So time complexity will be **O (n^2)**.

Binary Tree Sort

Binary tree sort uses a binary search tree (BST). In this algorithm, each element in the input list is inserted in a BST. During insertion the element being inserted is compared with nodes in the BST starting with the root node and moving towards the leaf nodes. If the element is less than node, then it is placed in the left branch, otherwise in the right branch. After all elements are inserted in the BST, it is traversed in in-order (left, root, right) to get the elements in ascending order.

Let's understand this in more details. Suppose **arr** is an array that consists of 10 distinct elements. The elements are as follows:

11, 2, 9, 13, 57, 25, 17, 1, 90, 3

The BST that can be built from these elements is shown in Figure 9-7.

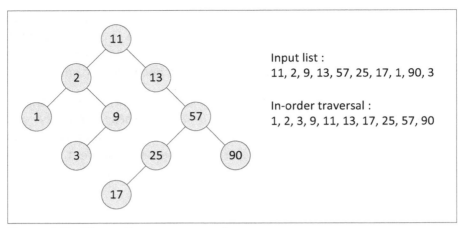

Input list :
11, 2, 9, 13, 57, 25, 17, 1, 90, 3

In-order traversal :
1, 2, 3, 9, 11, 13, 17, 25, 57, 90

Figure 9-7. *Binary Tree sort at work.*

The binary tree sort algorithm works as follows:

(a) To construct the binary search tree, we start with the 0th element 11. It is made the root of the tree.

(b) While inserting the 1st element, i.e. 2, 2 is compared with the root node 11. Since 2 is less than 11 it is made the left child of the root node 11.

(c) While inserting the 2nd element of the list, i.e. 13, it is compared with the root element 11. Since 13 is greater than 11 it is made the right child of the root node 11.

(d) Similarly, all other elements are placed in their proper position in the binary search tree.

(e) Now to get the elements in the sorted order, the tree is traversed in in-order and the elements are restored in the array.

The following program implements the binary tree sort algorithm.

Honest Solid Code   {C++}

Program 9-8. Implementation of Binary Tree Sort algorithm

```
#include <iostream>
using namespace std ;

struct btreenode
```

```
{
    struct btreenode *leftchild ;
    int data ;
    struct btreenode *rightchild ;
} ;

void binarytreesort ( int [ ], int ) ;
void insert ( struct btreenode **, int ) ;
void inorder ( struct btreenode *, int [ ], int * ) ;

int main( )
{
    int arr[ ] = { 11, 2, 9, 13, 57, 25, 17, 1, 90, 3 } ;
    int i ;

    cout << "Binary tree sort" << endl ;
    cout << "Array before sorting:" << endl ;
    for ( i = 0 ; i < 10 ; i++ )
        cout << arr[ i ] << "\t" ;

    binarytreesort ( arr, 10 ) ;

    cout << endl << "Array after sorting:" << endl ;
    for ( i = 0 ; i < 10 ; i++ )
        cout << arr[ i ] << "\t" ;

    return 0 ;
}

void binarytreesort ( int a[ ], int size )
{
    struct btreenode *bt ;
    int i ;

    bt = NULL ;
    for ( i = 0 ; i < size ; i++ )
        insert ( &bt, a[ i ] ) ;

    i = 0 ;
    inorder ( bt, a, &i ) ;
}
```

```
void insert ( struct btreenode **pr, int num )
{
    if ( *pr == NULL )
    {
        *pr = ( struct btreenode * ) malloc ( sizeof ( struct btreenode ) ) ;

        ( *pr )->leftchild = NULL ;
        ( *pr )->data = num ;
        ( *pr )->rightchild = NULL ;
    }
    else
    {
        if ( num < ( *pr )->data )
            insert ( &( ( *pr )->leftchild ), num ) ;
        else
            insert ( &( ( *pr )->rightchild ), num ) ;
    }
}

void inorder ( struct btreenode *pr, int a[ ], int *p )
{
    if ( pr != NULL )
    {
        inorder ( pr->leftchild, a, p ) ;
        a[ *p ] = pr->data ;
        *p = *p + 1 ;
        inorder ( pr->rightchild, a, p ) ;
    }
}
```

Output:

Binary Tree sort
Array before sorting:
11   2   9   13   57   25   17   1   90   3
Array after sorting:
1   2   3   9   11   13   17   25   57   90

The **binarytreesort( )** function calls **insert( )** function for each element in the array to construct the BST, and **inorder( )** function to visit the constructed BST in in-order fashion.

In the **insert( )** function it is ascertained whether BST is empty or not. If it is empty then a new node is created and the data to be inserted is stored in it. The left and right child of this new node is set with a **NULL** value, as this is the first node being inserted.

If BST is not empty then the current node is compared with the data to be inserted and **insert( )** function is called recursively to insert the node in the left/right sub-tree. Thus **insert( )** continues to move down the levels of BST until it reaches a leaf node. When it does, the new node gets inserted in the left/right sub-tree.

The **inorder( )** function receives address of the root node of BST, address of the array and an index where each visited element of BST should be inserted in the array. In the function a condition is checked whether the pointer is **NULL**. If the pointer is not **NULL** then a recursive call is made first for the left child and then for the right child. The values passed are the address of the left and right children that are present in the pointers **leftchild** and **rightchild** respectively. In between these two calls the data of the current node is stored in the array.

In binary tree sort there are two distinct steps—creation of BST and visiting it in in-order. The worst case will be if the array is already in sorted order. Let us discuss the time complexity in this case.

While constructing the BST, to insert 1st element of this array into BST we have to perform 1 comparison, to insert 2nd element we have to do 2 comparsions, to insert 3rd element we have to do 3 comparisons. So to insert **n** elements it has to do **n (n + 1) / 2** comparisons.

If there are **n** elements in the list there will be **n** nodes in the BST. While performing in-order traversal of the BST we perform maximum of 3 comparisons for any node. For n nodes the maximum number of comparisons will be **3n**.

So, total number of comparisons for this algorithm will be **n (n + 1) / 2 + 3 n**. Ignoring constants and lower order terms, time complexity of binary tree sort will be **O (n^2)**.

The drawback of the binary tree sort is that additional space is required for building the BST.

Merge Sort

Like Quick sort, Merge sort is also a recursive algorithm. It goes on splitting the array into sub-arrays till we get sub-arrays of size 1. Then it compares elements of 1-element sub-arrays to merge them into a 2-element sorted array. Then it merges two such 2-element sorted sub-arrays to build a 4-element sorted sub-array. This process continues up the ladder till we get a complete sorted array.

This merging process for two 5-element sorted sub-arrays is shown in Figure 9-8. In the first step elements 2 and 1 are compared. Of these, 1 is smaller. Hence it is transferred to the sorted array. Then 2 and 3 are compared, and so on. I think you get the picture now.

Note that, if during comparison end of one of the sub-arrays is reached, then the remaining elements from the other sub-array are copied into the third list.

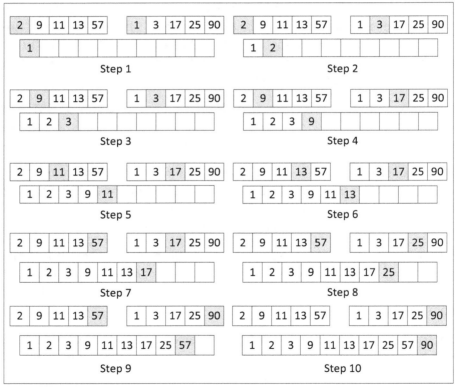

Figure 9-8. *Merge sort at work.*

The following program implements the merge sort algorithm.

Honest Solid Code

{C++}

Program 9-9. Implementation of Merge Sort algorithm

```cpp
#include <iostream>
using namespace std ;

void mergesort ( int [ ], int, int ) ;
void merge ( int [ ], int, int, int ) ;

int main( )
{
    int arr[ ] = { 11, 2, 9, 13, 57, 25, 17, 1, 90, 3 } ;
    int i ;

    cout << "Merge sort" << endl ;
    cout << "Array before sorting:" << endl ;
    for ( i = 0 ; i < 10 ; i++ )
        cout << arr[ i ] << "\t" ;

    mergesort ( arr, 0, 9 ) ;

    cout << endl << "Array after sorting:" << endl ;
    for ( i = 0 ; i < 10 ; i++ )
        cout << arr[ i ] << "\t" ;

    return 0 ;
}

void mergesort ( int a[ ], int lower, int upper )
{
    int mid ;

    if ( lower < upper )
    {
        mid = ( lower + upper ) / 2 ;
        mergesort ( a, lower, mid ) ;
        mergesort ( a, mid + 1, upper ) ;
        merge ( a, lower, mid, upper ) ;
    }
```

```
}

void merge ( int a[ ], int lower, int mid, int upper )
{
    int size, *b, first, second, idx, i ;

    size = upper - lower + 1 ;
    b = ( int * ) malloc ( size * sizeof ( int ) ) ;

    first = lower ;
    second = mid + 1 ;
    idx = 0 ;

    while ( first <= mid && second <= upper )
    {
        if ( a[ first ] <= a[ second ] )
        {
            b[ idx ] = a[ first ] ;
            first++ ; idx++ ;
        }
        else
        {
            b[ idx ] = a[ second ] ;
            second++ ; idx++ ;
        }
    }

    while ( first <= mid )
    {
        b[ idx ] = a[ first ] ;
        idx++ ;  first++ ;
    }

    while ( second <= upper )
    {
        b[ idx ] = a[ second ] ;
        idx++ ;  second++ ;
    }

    idx = 0 ;
    for ( i = lower ; i <= upper ; i++ )
```

```
    {
        a[ i ] = b[ idx ] ;
        idx++ ;
    }

    delete b ;
}
```

Output:

Merge sort
Array before sorting:
11   2   9   13   57   25   17   1   90   3
Array after sorting:
1   2   3   9   11   13   17   25   57   90

The logic of **merge( )** function is similar to the polynomial addition logic discussed in Chapter 2. The two sub-arrays being merged are part of the original array **arr[ ]**. They are identified as two separate sub-arrays using **lower**, **mid** and **upper**. The first sub-array is from index **lower** to **mid**, and the second from **mid + 1** to **upper**. For the purpose of merging another array **b[ ]** is created dynamically. Once array **b[ ]** contains the sorted elements, they are copied back into original array **arr[ ]** and the memory occupied by **b[ ]** is freed.

Suppose **arr[ ]** is an 8-element array. At level 1 we will split it into sub-arrays—**arr[0]** to **arr[3]** and **arr[4]** to **arr[7]**. At the next level, we will split the first sub-array into two sub-sub-arrays—one from **arr[0]** to **arr[1]** and second from **arr[2]** to **arr[3]**. So how many levels would we have if we are to reach 1-element sub-arrays? Well, it would be $\log_2$ **8**, or in general $\log_2$ **n**. At each level we are doing **n** comparisons for merging. So time complexity of merge sort algorithm would be **O (n $\log_2$ n)**.

Heap Sort

In this algorithm a binary heap is used. Recall from Chapter 7 that all levels of a binary heap are completely filled except perhaps last and at the last level nodes are as much to left as possible. In a **max-heap** the value at the root of any sub-tree is greater than or equal to the value of either of its sub-trees.

Heap sort is an improvement over the binary tree sort. Unlike a binary tree sort, it does not create a new binary tree from the input list. Instead it builds a heap by adjusting the position of elements within the array itself. Thus, it sorts the array in-place, without needing any extra space.

Given below are the steps involved in the heap sort algorithm.

(a) Build a max heap of array elements

(b) Swap Root element with last array element

(c) Build max heap excluding last element

(d) Decrease heap length by 1

(e) Repeat steps (b), (c), (d) until array gets sorted

Let us now understand this procedure with the help of an example. Suppose an array contains elements 11, 2, 9, 13, 57, 25, 17, 1, 90, and 3. A binary heap representation of this array is shown in Figure 9-8. To convert this binary heap into a max-heap we need to repeatedly heapify the nodes in it. While heapifying a node in a max heap, we need to ensure that all its children satisfy the heap property—Parent >= Left child, Right child. This operation involves following steps:

(a) Pick maximum out of given node, and its left and right child

(b) If maximum is root, do nothing

(c) If maximum is left, exchange root with left and heapify left node

(d) If maximum is right, exchange root with right and heapify right node

These operations are shown in Figure 9-9.

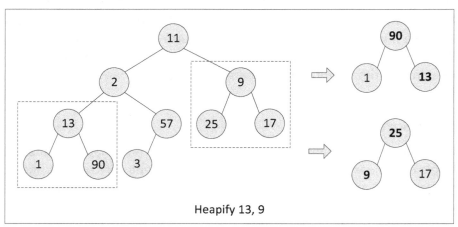

Heapify 13, 9

Figure 9-9. *Heapify operation.*

Note that in the binary tree shown in Figure 9-9 node 13 and node 9 are violating the heap property, so we need to heapify them. While heapifying 13, maximum out of 13, 1, and 90 is 90. Since 90 is the right child it is exchanged with 13. As against this, while heapifying 9, maximum (25) turns out to be the left child. So 25 is exchanged with 9. Since after exchange 13 and 9 became child nodes, we did not have to heapify them further.

The following program implements the heap sort algorithm:

Honest Solid Code   {C++}

Program 9-10. Implementation of Heap Sort algorithm

```cpp
#include <iostream>
using namespace std ;

void heapsort ( int [ ], int ) ;
void heapify ( int [ ], int, int ) ;

int main( )
{
    int arr[ ] = { 11, 2, 9, 13, 57, 25, 17, 1, 90, 3 } ;
    int i ;

    cout << "Heap sort" << endl ;
    cout << "Array before sorting:" << endl ;
    for ( i = 0 ; i < 10 ; i++ )
        cout << arr[ i ] << "\t" ;

    heapsort ( arr, 10 ) ;

    cout << endl << "Array after sorting:" << endl ;
    for ( i = 0 ; i < 10 ; i++ )
        cout << arr[ i ] << "\t" ;

    return 0 ;
}

void heapsort ( int a[ ], int n )
{
```

```
    int i, t ;

    /* create max heap */
    for ( i = n / 2 - 1 ; i >= 0 ; i-- )
        heapify ( a, n, i ) ;

    for ( i = n - 1 ; i >= 0 ; i-- )
    {
        /* move current root to end */
        t = a[ 0 ] ;
        a[ 0 ] = a[ i ] ;
        a[ i ] = t ;

        /* heapify the reduced heap */
        heapify ( a, i, 0 ) ;
    }
}

void heapify ( int a[ ], int sz, int i )
{
    int largest, lch, rch, t ;

    lch = 2 * i + 1 ;
    rch = 2 * i + 2 ;

    if ( lch >= sz )
        return ;

    largest = i ;

    /* if left child is larger than root */
    if ( lch < sz && a[ lch ] > a[ largest ] )
        largest = lch ;

    /* if right child is larger than largest so far */
    if ( rch < sz && a[ rch ] > a[ largest ] )
        largest = rch ;

    /* if largest is not root */
    if ( largest != i )
    {
```

```
        t = a[ i ] ;
        a[ i ] = a[ largest ] ;
        a[ largest ] = t ;

        /* heapify the affected sub-tree */
        heapify ( a, sz, largest ) ;
    }
}
```

Output:

```
Heap sort
Array before sorting:
11   2   9   13   57   25   17   1   90   3
Array after sorting:
1   2   3   9   11   13   17   25   57   90
```

The program begins by declaring an array that represents the binary tree. We know that in array representation of a binary tree, a node at location **i** has its left and right child at locations **(2i + 1)** and **(2i + 2)** respectively.

Next, in the **heapsort( )** function in a **for** loop we have repeatedly called **heapify( )** moving level by level from leaf towards root, and at any level from right to left, starting from node at location **size / 2 - 1**. The **heapify( )** function finds the largest out of given node, and its left and right child. If the given node turns out to be largest then it does nothing. But if left/right child turns out to be largest it exchanges the given node with left/right child and then proceeds to heapify the left/right child.

Note that in the program we do not physically construct this binary tree by establishing the link between the nodes. Instead, we imagine this tree and then readjust the array elements to form a heap.

Once the max-heap is created the current root node is moved to the end and **heapify( )** is called once again to heapify the reduced heap.

Let us now analyze the time complexity of heap sort algorithm. For this we must first consider the time complexity of **heapify( )** function. In the worst case, while heapifying a value it does $\log_2 n$ comparisons. This is equal to the height of a complete binary tree. Since we are calling this function **n** times in **heapsort( )**, the time complexity of heap sort algorithm will be **O (n $\log_2$ n)**.

Chapter Bullets

Summary of chapter

(a) Searching an element in a list can be done using linear search or binary search algorithm.

(b) Binary search algorithm is more efficient than linear search algorithm.

(c) Binary search algorithm expects the elements of a list in ascending order.

(d) Binary search can be done iteratively or recursively.

(e) Internal sorting is used when the input data can be accommodated in memory.

(f) External sorting is used when data is so huge that all of it cannot be stored in memory at a time.

(g) Common internal sorting algorithms include bubble sort, selection sort, insertion sort, quick sort, merge sort, binary tree sort and heap sort.

Check Your Progress

Exercise - Level I

[A] State whether the following statements are True or False:

(a) Sorting is the method of arranging a list of elements in a particular order.

(b) Linear search is more efficient than the binary search.

(c) Merge sort needs additional space to sort an array.

(d) Binary tree sort needs additional space to sort an array.

(e) Time complexity of Quick sort is **O (n log$_2$ n)**.

(f) Insertion sort is more efficient than Heap sort.

Sharpen Your Skills

Exercise - Level II

[B] Answer the Following:

(a) What is the difference between an internal sorting and external sorting?

(b) Write a program that determines the first occurrence of a given sub-array within it.

Coding Interview Questions

Exercise Level III

[C] Answer the Following:

(a) Suppose an array contains **n** elements. Given a number **x** that may occur several times in the array. Find

    — the number of occurrences of **x** in the array

    — the position of first occurrence of **x** in the array.

(b) Write a program that implements insertion sort algorithm for a linked list of integers.

(c) Write a program that sorts the elements of a two-dimensional array row wise / column wise.

Case Scenario Exercise

External Sorting

External sorting is useful for sorting huge amount of data that cannot be accommodated in the memory all at a time. So data from the disk is loaded into memory part by part and each part that is loaded is sorted and the sorted data is stored into some intermediate file. Finally, all the sorted parts present in different intermediate files are merged into one single file.

Initially the original file (file number 1) is partitioned into two files (file number 2 and 3). Then one item is read from each file (file number 2 and 3) and the two items are written in sorted order in a new file (file number 4). Once again one item is read from each partitioned files (file number 2 and 3) and these two items are written in sorted order in another new file (file number 5). Thus alternate pair of sorted items are stored in the file number 4 and 5. This procedure is repeated till the partitioned files (file number 2 and 3) come to an end.

Now following procedure is repeated twice:

(a) Read one item from file number 4 and 5 and write them in sorted order in file number 2.

(b) Read one item from file number 4 and 5 and write them in sorted order in file number 3.

Note that instead of creating two new files, the partitioned files (2 and 3) are being reused.

After this the following procedure is repeated 4 times:

(a) Read one item from file number 2 and 3 and write them in sorted order in file number 4.

(b) Read one item from file number 2 and 3 and write them in sorted order in file number 5.

In this way alternately items are moved from a pair of partitioned files to the pair of new files and from pair of new files to a pair of partitioned files. This procedure is repeated till the time we do not end up writing entire data in a single file. When this happens all the items in this file would be in sorted order.

Write a program that implements the external sort algorithm.

Index

Search It Out

How to use the Downloadable DVD

Since these days most laptops do not have a DVD drive, we haven't enclosed the DVD with the book. Instead its contents have been made available for download. They can be downloaded using any one of the following links:

https://drive.google.com/drive/folders/1BLV2QtOmkCd70WQrU2ebr BcpOciMAF7U

OR

http://bit.ly/2VjEwiu

Download all the files shown when you visit this link.

Once downloaded, you can install the contents by double-clicking the file CDStart.exe. Follow the instructions that will appear on the screen.

Once the installation is over you can access the animations as well as the sample programs.